Frederick Soddy

The Rôle of Money
What it should be, contrasted with what it has become

ⒺMNIA VERITAS®

Frederick Soddy
(1877–1956)

English chemist and recipient
of the 1921 Nobel Prize for Chemistry

The Rôle of Money
What it should be, contrasted with what it has become

First edition, London: George Routledge & Sons Ltd, 1934

© Omnia Veritas Ltd - 2021

ISBN: 978-1-913890-52-0

Published by
Omnia Veritas Ltd

*⊘*MNIA VERITAS®

www.omnia-veritas.com

PREFACE

This book attempts to clear up the mystery of money in its social aspect. With the monetary system of the whole world in chaos, this mystery has never been so carefully fostered as it is today. And this is all the more curious inasmuch as there is not the slightest reason for this mystery. This book will show what money now is, what it does, and what it should do. From this will emerge the recognition of what has always been the true role of money. The standpoint from which most books on modern money are written has been reversed. In this book the subject is not treated from the point of view of the bankers – as those are called who create by far the greater proportion of money – but from that of the PUBLIC, who at present have to give up valuable goods and services to the bankers in return for the money that they have so cleverly created and create. This, surely, is what the public really wants to know about money.

It was recognized in Athens and Sparta ten centuries before the birth of Christ that one of the most vital prerogatives of the State was the sole right to issue money. How curious that the unique quality of this prerogative is only now being rediscovered. The "money-power" which has been able to overshadow ostensibly responsible government, is not the power of the merely ultrarich, but is nothing more nor less than a new technique designed to create and destroy money by adding and withdrawing figures in bank ledgers, without the slightest concern for the interests of the community or the real rôle that money ought to perform therein.

The more profound students of money and, more recently, a very few historians have realized the enormous significance of this money power or technique, and its key position in shaping the course of world events through the ages. In this book the mode of approach and the philosophy of money is expounded in the light of a group of new doctrines, to which the name *ergosophy* is collectively given, which regard economics, sociology, and history with the eye of the engineer rather than with that of the humanist. It is concerned less with the details of particular schemes of monetary reform that have been advocated than with the general principles to which, in the author's opinion, every monetary system must at long last conform, if it is to fulfil its proper rôle as the distributive mechanism of society. To allow it to become a source of revenue to private issuers is to create, first, a secret and illicit arm of the government and, last, a rival power strong enough ultimately to overthrow all other forms of government.

CHAPTER I

THE PHILOSOPHICAL BACKGROUND – ERGOSOPHY

THE Objective

It is now some sixteen years since the close of the great event that displayed, for all to see, man and his would-be rulers and mentors powerless in the grip of the forces that their technologists had safely chained but that war had let loose. There is a distinct understanding in the general consciousness that this generation is witnessing the veritable birth-throes of a new era dictated by the progress of physical science, rather than owing anything to those who have hitherto been most vocal in debate or most prominent in the attempted direction of affairs. There is a growing exasperation that an age so splendid and full of the noblest promise of generous life should be in such ill-informed and incompetent hands.

The Monetary System Obsolete

Everywhere now there is the dawning consciousness among thoughtful minds that this age contains elements not understood or contained within the working rules of the older systems of government, economics, sociology, or even religion, and that it is due to new principles that have to be introduced into the base and can in no wise be met by a change in the superstructure of society. Even more remarkable, almost incredibly so to those who have been hitherto lost voices crying in the wilderness, is the swiftly growing volume of agreement that it is the obsolete and dangerous monetary system that, primarily, is at fault. It is this entirely empirical and defeatist body of rules and conventions, that has grown up along with the scientific expansion of the means of life, that is responsible not only for the present paralysis but also for the Great War itself. All are agreed that here at least change is inevitable, the only doubt indeed now being whether any part of the system, which through a lack of imagination as to what might have been is still apt to be described as having "worked well in the past", can survive into the future.

The present book as dealing with cannot fail therefore to be of fundamental importance, if it succeeds at all in filling its place in the New World Series, which is nothing less than to be a guide and a lamp to those whom fate shall select to be the new leaders of the great, though not of necessity violent, changes that are close upon us. When the war forced upon everybody's attention the grave dangers surrounding a scientific civilization through the very immensity of the destructive powers that science has put into the hands of nations. Still thinking only in terms of brute strength, the writer undertook an original examination into the real physical foundations of the conventions and half-truths that pass for economics, and particularly into those underlying the mechanism of distribution, which is, in a monetary civilization, the money system. His most significant conclusion, from which subsequent events have given him no reason to recede, – indeed it is now a truism – was that nothing useful can be done unless and until a scientific money system takes the place of the one now always breaking down.

The corollary, however, is never likely to be popular with our professional politicians at least. It was that, if such a thing were done, little else in the way of arbitrary interference with and government control over the essential activities of men in the pursuit of their livelihood would be required. Indeed, just as now not one in a thousand understands why the existing money system has such power to hurt him, so, if it were corrected as here outlined, not one in a thousand would need to know or, indeed, would know, except by the consequences, either that it had been rectified or how it had been rectified. For the aim of the present book is to show how the money system may be reduced to one of exactly the same character as that of our standard weights and measures.

The Community Standpoint

It will be necessary to go more fully into the combination of circumstances which make these matters at once so vital to the social and economic health of the community and so completely outside the ways of thought that appertain to the individual and guide him in his own private affairs. Much of the difficulty is of course the deliberate use hitherto of common terms in senses entirely novel and often the opposite of those normally meant, as for example *cash* and *credit*. Much also is due to misconception as to what undoubtedly constitutes wealth to an individual, when not the individual but the community is in question. Because of this, the technical study of money calls in a peculiar way for powers of generalization, and often, indeed, the complete inversion of ideas as they appertain to the individual. These factors have unfortunately been completely absent not only from so-called monetary science but to an equal and even more important extent from the fundamental systems of orthodox economics to which monetary science belongs.

Now, born of the troubled times in which we live, there has been growing up from a number of independent and at first sight quite unconnected roots a group of doctrines which may be broadly described as the application of the principles of the sciences of the material world, physics and chemistry, to economics and sociology. They have a common feature in that they are all due to the original thought of scientific men – mainly engineers and physical scientists – more interested in and accustomed to think in terms of physical realities than in those of social or legal conventions, and concerned hardly at all with the problems and controversies of individual or class economics, but with the significance of broad general and completely inescapable principles, in particular the principles of energetics, in regard to welfare of whole communities as affected by the production and distribution of wealth.

Social Importance of Energetics

In the author's opinion, at least, this new development promises to be of far more ultimate and permanent importance to the science of human welfare than the earlier incursion of biology in the last century which led to the doctrine of evolution. This is because it imposes a rigid framework of the fundamental physical laws, applying equally to men as to machines, in which there is really nothing controversial at all. The stock criticism of such a mode of approach into sociological questions would have been that men are not machines, and that in economics, as in its subdivision, money, psychological factors and considerations are at least of equal importance to, if indeed they are not of greater importance than, the purely physical factors.

But that argument, unless it frankly postulates a belief in physical miracles – in the power of the human mind to make, if it so will, 2 + 2 = 5 – whatever it may once have been, is now largely out of date through the extension of the exact sciences into these fields. There is not, never has been, and perhaps never will be any sort of equality at all in importance between the physical and psychological. In the sphere of distribution, for example, or of money as the distributory mechanism, all that psychology can do – and the same is equally true of "banking" as it has become – is to rob Peter to pay Paul.

Energy Theory of Wealth

One of the main contributions of these doctrines is a consistent energy theory of wealth and the sharp distinction that results between wealth and the ownership of a debt. This reveals much that is incontrovertible regarding the threatened collapse of the modern scientific civilization, to give it its proper name, though it is usually miscalled the capitalistic civilization. True, "Capital," in its proper physical sense, is its most distinctive superficial feature. But in that sense Capital is the unconsumable product of the irrevocable consumption or expenditure of wealth necessary to prepare for and make possible the new methods of production. Owing to modern methods of power production, much more of it is necessary than with the old methods. Moreover, it may be exchangeable for fresh wealth, but it is not changeable into it. From the community's standpoint capital appears as debt rather than wealth.

Orthodox economics has never yet been anything but the class economics of the owners of debts. If its writers ever attempted any wider social applications, they made themselves simply ridiculous, as when one solemnly looked forward to the millennium arriving through the accumulation of so much capital that everyone would be well off and comfortable, presumably by living on the interest of their mutual indebtednesses. Whilst in the sphere of international trade, till long after the war, the dictum that a continued favourable balance of trade was essential for the existence of the strong nations implied the continuation of unfavourable balances for the weak. It was stated that this country was threatened with disaster unless it contrived to maintain the previous rate of foreign investments – returning abroad all that it received in the way of interest and sinking funds in respect of past investments, and if possible more than this. These are good illustrations of the debt-view of wealth and the substitution of social and legal conventions for physical reality.

Ergosophy

It is convenient to give a name to the group of interconnected but more or less independent doctrines comprised under such terms as Cartesian, Physical or New Economics, Social Energetics, the Age of Plenty, and Technocracy, including the implications of these doctrines, in regard to the problems of distribution and the new philosophy of money, with which this book is more particularly concerned. A new word Ergosophy will be employed for this purpose. It means the wisdom of work, energy, or power, in the purely physical sense. Mental or intellectual activities, to which these three terms are often loosely applied, are better referred to, rather, as effort, diligence, or attention.

There are many reasons that render such a new word or term desirable. So far there has been no real social philosophy arising wholly out of the universally obeyed laws of the physical world. On the other hand, from the remotest times, technology has been too apt to be considered merely a sort of slave or menial servant to verbose, pretentious, and impressionistic humane philosophies and religions. Indeed it would hardly be a caricature of civilization, as it has evolved up to now, to describe it as having been attempting to compound for the injustice of ascribing unto God the things that are of Science by rendering unto Caesar the things that are of God. Technocracy, in one at least of its sources of inspiration, the suggestion of Thorstein Veblen for the establishment of a Soviet of technicians to take over the control of the world, is probably one of the first collective dawnings of this malversation. So long as we have simple folk displaying a pathetic acquiescence in the piety that renders thanks for all the good things of life and ascribes them to the bounty of Providence, along with anything but simple folk who totally disbelieve anything of the kind but nevertheless do still believe implicitly in practising much more forceful methods of obtaining them, so long will civilization be a happy hunting ground for the predatory and acquisitive and a wilderness for the original and creative. The new philosophy, by claiming for mechanical science its rightful position as an equal in the trinity of wisdom, should make it easier to render unto

Caesar the things that are of Caesar and to God the things that are of God.

Wealth and Calories

In the first place ergosophy rehabilitates with a precise meaning that old-fashioned and indispensable word *Wealth*, which the orthodox economist, knowing even less of the alleged subject-matter of his studies than the original founders of the subject, the French Physiocrats, took too much for granted. Originating, to him, ultimately somehow through divine agency, he came to regard the acquisition of wealth as tantamount to its creation. He became obsessed with commerce and mercantile exchange to the neglect of the technical principles underlying all new production of wealth. To this day we are in the grip of a mercantile system that fritters away in distribution most of the advantage gained in lightening the labour of producing wealth. Involved in a mass of obvious inconsistencies, he seemed to resent the use of the term wealth at all by those unlearned in his sophistications. Even the orthodox are today exceedingly sparing in the use of the word. The discussion that has lately been greatly in evidence in the papers as to the income necessary to purchase, among other things, sufficient food to support a family in health and work possesses a significance that may perhaps have been missed. The whole question centred round the number of calories of energy contained in the food itself, this to be proved, if necessary, by burning it in a calorimeter. This is economics, even if it is not yet recognized as such.

Marxism Obsolete

It ought never to be forgotten that Victorian economics was essentially class economics, in which only gradually and tardily the actual producers of wealth as distinct from employers and property owners were considered at all. But we find things worse and not better among the accepted doctrines of left-wing and revolutionary movements. With a clearer recognition of the social implications of energy our political controversies appear mainly as due to economic confusions. In an age when men are more and more being displaced from their function as physical labourers by purely inanimate sources of power, and are in danger of being largely by-passed out of the cycle of production and distribution by automatic mechanisms, it would be incredible, if it were not true, that so large a part of the world should be misrepresented as dominated by the doctrines of Karl Marx as to wealth originating in *human* labour. Every artisan must know that this is not now true. The views of Marx on money were even more out of date, relatively to his age, than his views on wealth, and it was significant in the evidence before the Macmillan Committee that Marxists seem to have been the last to abandon their primitive belief in gold as a currency medium and in the gold standard.

Relations between Peoples and Governments

If, as appears to be happening, these obsolete ideas and the doctrinaires who exploit them are rapidly losing their hold on the public, and if an increasing body of people of all shades of political opinion are wakening to the more fundamental revolutions rendered inescapable by the progress of science, it is possible to anticipate for this and other countries not yet overtaken by revolution a very different and more reasonable, if more prosaic, course of events. For it is no progress, having absolved the Deity from the function of universal provider, to set up the Government in His place. Veblen was much nearer the reality in substituting the technologist. In the economic affairs of the nation, at least, it would seem no bad thing if the ordinary practical rules of business were followed, success and honesty being encouraged by promotion, and incompetence and corruption entailing dismissal much as with any other paid officials.

Physical Interpretation of History

Nor does history seem able to escape from much the same charge as economics. If, in other revolutions, we study not the actions and loudly proclaimed motives of the contending parties but rather the permanent and abiding fruits of the struggle, there appears little if any resemblance. Historians seem open to the charge of recording rather what ought to have been happening according to their one-sided philosophic preconceptions, than what really happened. Actually, the successive political factions appear to have gone on effectually cancelling each other out until, by a process of elimination, the new factors in the world which permitted and, indeed, enforced a more satisfying and intelligent mode of living were given freer play. Then, and then only, the ferment subsided.

This, at least, is the interpretation of history by Sydney A. Reeve, an American engineer who has for thirty years been devoting himself to the study of the great historic wars and revolutions of the past, from the standpoint of Social Energetics. His conclusion that these terrible and devastating explosions could have been avoided, and can in the future be prevented, is, obviously, of prime importance in the present state of the world. Human aspirations towards progress may be taken for granted. Even in total eclipse they are not dead, but only latent. But whether they can achieve realization rather than mere passive or active revolt, doomed in advance to futility, is in the end a question of the physical resources rather than the psychical attitudes of men. Without an abundance, all the more essential because of the destruction these outbursts entail, the most valiant and heroic strivings are vain.

The Truth about "Materialism"

This may sound like sordid and unrelieved materialism, and may have an ominous ring in the ears of many. Yet nothing but ignorance or worse could make it appear so. It is better to listen to those who have made the desert blossom as the rose rather than to those who have made fair fields a slime of mud and blood; to those who have fetched from the stars the cornucopia that suckled Jupiter instead of those who empty it in the rivers and the fire for fear of glut; to those who would let light and air into warrens and fight social disease with food and warmth rather than drugs and doles; who wait to loose into life the mounting tide of wealth rather than watch it burst its dams and leap again to the work of destruction and death. Rather is it not terrible that men who can do all these things are reckoned the mere hirelings of miscalled humanists and idealists, and are not supposed to be concerned whether they are hired to create or destroy! Even the mules of the United States, we read, when the boll-weevils, specially imported for the purpose, failed to destroy the cotton crop to prevent "overproduction", refused to tread back into the earth the growing plants. Whereas men, with resources at their disposal ample to build up a civilization of a magnificence and liberality the world has never known, are now at their wit's end to invent new forms of destruction and waste lest this new civilization should displace the old.

The Physical Origin of "Progress"

Some may see in ergosophy nothing but economic determinism pushed to extremes. True, calories are king all right in the sense that nothing whatever can happen without sufficient expenditure of them, a condition upon which humanists usually find it convenient not to dwell. But this sort of determinism the new doctrine deduces to laws which do not arise from life at all, though all life obeys them. That this is not – or at least was not – merely trite and self-evident is clear from the views of Marx, to whom the doctrine of economic determinism is so largely ascribed, as to the origin of wealth. If he had left out from his definition of wealth the word "human", and had said that wealth had originated in labour, in the sense the physicist uses the word for work or energy, he would have anticipated modern views. Instead, he referred to the original founder of this, perhaps the greatest of all scientific generalizations, as "an American humbug, the baronized Yankee, Benjamin Thompson, *alias* Count Rumford".

But though now this be little more than a truism, there is something much more positive in these doctrines than the mere barring out or subordination of human and religious factors from the ultimate arbitrament of the fate of communities. So far as the individual goes there appears perfect free-will to utilize or not the opportunities afforded by invention and discovery in order to lighten the labour and multiply the rewards of livelihood. But this free-will by no means extends to his ability permanently to prevent others from so doing. Reeve's theory of wars and revolutions is that they arise from just this attempt, which is always ultimately unsuccessful and disastrous. Whatever you may choose to label the new view, it implies clearly that human progress is predestined from below, even if not initiated from above. At the best men may be led on to higher modes of life, but at the worst they are impelled from the rear. But it leaves, as outside its province, the actual form and nature of human progress to the other members of the trinity, the biological and psychical content of the age that may be in existence at the time.

The Doctrine of Struggle

Unpleasant and shattering to many cherished illusions as this may seem, it is, nevertheless, the key that best fits our age, and none know it better than those who have tried to spread the new evangel. As an Australian writer recently well put it – there are many who cling to (for others not themselves) poverty, insecurity, hard work, scanty living, wars, starvation, and disease, as blessings in disguise, necessary to goad and subdue this lazy and unruly animal, man, and to protect him from softness and decadence. This is the doctrine of existence for struggle, rather than of struggle for existence, and it is probably the oldest doctrine in the world. It stinks of the East not the West. If it is regarded as "biological necessity", the physical imperative is even more categorical. For in struggle man can not now exist – he can only destroy himself and be destroyed. Surely it is rather crude biology, seeing that from its earliest inception life has been doing little else than dodge physical imperatives, to suppose that man should at this epoch of his evolution suddenly reverse his instincts and, of necessity, knock out his brains against them. In truth, these ideas have, as the Australian writer was careful to point out, only a vicarious application, and the biological necessity of death for the individual is still the greatest insurance for the survival of the species. The problem is, rather, educational – for the race to learn effectively to protect itself against those who, learned mainly in the history of the bygone bow and arrow ages, would use the titanic weapons of science for race annihilation.

Men, it is true, in those ages may have been goaded on by starvation to successful robbery and theft of their neighbours, but, in this powerage, progress has been due to the conquest of nature and the by-passing of men. Whatever may be the ultimate genic effect of the Great War, it is generally admitted that the French Revolution and the Napoleonic Wars have perceptibly reduced the average physique of the French nation, and that now wars, since superior courage and valour are much more likely to lead to swift personal annihilation than ultimate survival, are definitely and necessarily dysgenic. While on the positive side, where courage and stamina are essential to survival, in exploration of land, sea, and sky, and in trying out and taming still imperfectly understood new processes and appliances to the use of men, science has provided and is providing both opportunities and unavoidable necessities for facing and overcoming dangers that would have blenched the cheek of the legendary heroes of olden time. The fault, if any, is rather with our poets for not suitably immortalizing such achievements, but in that field no one doubts the immense superiority of the ancients over us, who in so many other respects have very little to learn from them.

Modern Wars and National Debts

In point of fact, again, are wars now merely for sustenance? Are they not waged to secure markets wherein to dispose of the surplus wealth arising from scientific production operating along with the old practical law of wages? (By "practical law of wages" is meant the system that ensures to the worker just sufficient to maintain him in a mental and physical condition to allow of his efficient conduct of his trade, craft, or avocation. This is, of course, a *direct* inheritance of the age of scarcity.) To put it quite bluntly, the purpose of wars is to compel weaker nations to take this surplus off the hands of the stronger, running up debts, if need be, in order to pay for it. Then, the threat of further war is necessary to ensure that the debts and the interest on them shall not be repudiated.

The Real Struggles

The struggle for existence is now revealed as fundamentally a struggle for physical energy, and the conquest of nature has made available supplies vastly exceeding what can be extracted from the unwilling bodies of draught cattle and slaves. It is not the struggle but the energy that is essential to human life. The doctrine of existence for struggle, on the other hand, is the oldest religion in the world.

It has never been anything but a religion of the ambitious, dominating, and unscrupulous, with either a race or a caste arrogation of superiority over the races without or the herd within, an assumption of licence to act treacherously and injuriously towards aliens and those it deems of inferior breed and to confine its standards of honour and decency to those of its own blood or order. It is a code that Christianity has actively and passively resisted for two thousand years. That fact is not unimportant. For between the progress that has culminated in ergosophy and the Christian religion there is an intimate connection. Indeed the former is in origin wholly the product of the Christian nations of the West.

The Taboo on Scientific Economics

After the war, a cry went up for scientific men to cooperate with the financial, industrial, and political authorities in solving the social evils that brought on the war and which have since made Peace nothing but a misnomer. But the strange and unconventional conclusions of the few who had brought to social problems the same searching and original thought that they were accustomed to apply in their own inquiries, frightened, not the public, but those whose interest in such problems is to keep them reconciled with things as they are. Those who persisted in shedding light on social evils and anomalies were deemed impious, and the conclusions tabooed. But it is the merest folly to suppose that in these days any sweeping generalization that clarifies existing great issues can be suppressed. Now that there are signs that the Age of Plenty school of monetary reformers is winning, and that the conspiracy of silence on the part of the "respectable" Press has failed, we may assess the cost. Fifteen years of golden opportunity have been wasted, the time having been devoted instead to the exacerbation of the disease. Policies, which now everyone knows were the exact opposite of those required by the facts, such as economizing, or producing more and consuming less, have worked themselves out to their inevitable results. The public is expected to believe that the misfortunes that beset us are acts of God and that, though we have the science and the necessary equipment and organization to produce wealth in abundance, it is beyond the wit of man to learn how to distribute it. The problem, it is true, is new, and the approach to it obscured, often intentionally, by a mass of half-truths and once-truths. But its solution has not been rendered any nearer or clearer by the puerile effort of the post-War era to suppress free public discussion of the new doctrines, an issue that was fought out and won in physical science in the time of Galileo.

Wars and Revolutions Result from Wealth

The reader will no doubt be able to supply for himself many striking confirmations of the theory that wars and revolution result not from poverty and misery but from the growth of wealth and the futile attempt to resist its distribution. But two striking ones that occur to the author may be here cited. The first is as to the immediate and incidental causes that precipitated the first Kerensky Revolution in Russia. We were told by intelligent and unbiassed Russians at the time that it was neither starvation and poverty nor the horrors of defeat in war but two exhibitions of official incompetence so gross as to outrage the deepest feelings of Russia. The one was the mass conscription of the peasants long before there were arms or barracks for a small fraction of them, whereby a large proportion died from the pestilential conditions engendered. Even from a purely military standpoint they would have been far better left at work on their fields. The other was the loss of practically the whole of one season's crop of one of the chief grain districts of South Russia during transference from barges to the rail-head through its being dumped at a spot universally known as being liable to sudden autumn floods.

The second illustration is of more than incidental purport, Olive Schreiner in the introduction to her book *Woman and Labour* tells how she came to regard it as almost axiomatic that "the women of no race or class will ever revolt or attempt to bring about a revolutionary adjustment of their relation to their society, however intense their suffering and however clear their perception of it, while the welfare and persistence of their society requires their submission", they do so, in brief, when the changed conditions make acquiescence no longer necessary or desirable.

It is not suffering but *unnecessary* suffering and misery that is the goad of human progress. Precedent to the latter is the material progress in the inventions and arts that give men power over their environment, and happy indeed is the age in which precedent also, and keeping pace with the expansion of wealth, is progress in the moral and spiritual sphere. For then we get not revolution but renaissance. So in our day it is not the agitator fomenting class-hatred who can start, nor the airmen raining down bombs that can stop, a revolution. But empty milk into the Potomac; import pests to destroy the cotton crop; burn wheat and coffee as fuel; restrict the production of rubber; set up tariff-barriers; permit trusts, federations, cartels, and lock-outs; allow trade unions to develop ca'canny methods to reduce output; maintain in misery, insecurity, and idleness masses of unemployed who are not allowed to better their lot by making the very things of which they stand in need; and revolution in some form is not probable, but certain. The ideas that govern men are outraged. Instead of a few striking illustrations of incompetence or worse they begin to see universal chaos instead of order. Their institutions, so far from protecting them in their peaceful avocations on which they rely for their livelihood, appear leagued together to keep them in traditional and unnecessary servitude and dependence. The army begins to realize that it is officered by the enemy.

The Monetary System Impedes the Flow

Nor will any means avail to terminate or defeat such a revolution, whether it is sudden or long-drawn-out, violent or chronic, unless and until the barriers that oppose the free and full distribution of wealth from the producer to the ultimate user and consumer are broken down and the flow of wealth again fulfils the purpose for which men have striven to create it. Since, in all monetary civilizations, it is money that alone can effect the exchange of wealth and the continuous flow of goods and services throughout the nation, money has become the life-blood of the community, and for each individual a veritable licence to live at all. The monetary system is the distributory mechanism, and this reading of history therefore supports up to the hilt the conclusions of those who have made a special study of what our monetary system has become. It is the primary and infinitely most important source of all our present social and international unrest and for the failure, hitherto, of democracy.

A very slight knowledge of our actual existing monetary system makes it abundantly clear that, without democracy knowing or allowing it, and without the matter ever being before the electorate even as a secondary or minor political issue, the power of uttering money has been taken out of national hands and usurped as a prerequisite by the moneylender. Practically every genuine monetary reformer is unanimous that the only hope of safety and peace lies in the nation instantly resuming its prerogative over the issue of all forms of money, which, legally, it has never surrendered at all.

CHAPTER II

THE THEORY OF MONEY –
VIRTUAL WEALTH

WHAT is Money?

Let us commence our "study" of by a comprehensive definition of what modern money is.

Money now is the NOTHING *you get for* SOMETHING *before you can get* ANYTHING.

Our task is to understand all that this implies. The definition is, of course, an economic one referring to ordinary transactions such as earning, buying, and selling among ordinary folk – generous uncles and other voluntary benefactors not being under contemplation – and the *nothing, something,* and *anything* of the definition refer to things of real value in themselves, usually termed goods and services, or simply wealth, unless hair-splitting or purely technical distinctions turning on the precise definition of wealth are involved. Moreover, it refers to ordinary people, in the sense of those who neither have the opportunity nor the power of uttering money themselves.

As a matter of fact, this definition not only answers comprehensively what money now is but answers perfectly satisfactorily all that money has always been, whether it has been coin or paper or any other form. From the point of view of the owner or possessor of it, money is the credit he has established in his favour with the community in which it passes current or is "legal tender", by having *given up* in the past valuable goods and services for nothing, so as to obtain at his own convenience, in the future, equivalent value in turn for nothing. It is merely an ingenious device to secure payment in advance, and in a monetary civilization the owners of money are those who have paid in advance for definite market values of buyable goods and services, without as yet having received them.

There is nothing mysterious about all this. What has been termed "the moral mystery of credit", meaning credit-money, might just as well be termed the immoral mystery of debt. For there is no credit without debt any more than there is height without depth. East without West, or heat without cold. The two are related, and although it takes only one to own wealth it takes two to own a debt, because for every owner there is an ower. Money, of course, is an entirely peculiar form of the credit-debt relation, if only because whereas all other forms are entirely optional, the creditor at any rate being a free agent to enter into this relation or not, money is a credit-debt relation from which none can effectually escape.

Let us right from the start get the signs right. *The owner of money is the creditor* and the issuer of it is the debtor, for the owner of money gives up goods and services to the issuer. In an honest money system the issuer of money who gets for nothing goods and services would do so on trust for the benefit of the community. In a fraudulent money system he does so for the benefit of himself. It makes no difference whether he passes off the money and puts it into circulation himself or lends it at interest for others to pass off for him. In every case what he so gets to spend or lend is given up by someone else. *Ex nihilo nihil fit*. Nothing comes from nothing, or, in modern phraseology, matter and energy are conserved.

Barter and Barter-Currencies

The invention of money marks a distinct step upwards in civilization. In barter the owner of one sort of property gives it up to another in exchange for another sort of equivalent worth. Money was able to replace barter not because it enabled people to obtain other peoples' property without giving anything up, but because they had in a former and independent transaction already given it up. All the shades of distinction which money in the course of its evolution has passed through, from barter to pure credit (or debt), concern not the something initially given up for it, which is the one essential to all its forms. They concern merely what is received in exchange for it. This may vary from the full value in the form of a gold coin to an intrinsically worthless paper receipt, and nowadays not even that. For a variety of alleged reasons, such as the necessity to make money circulate freely, which we need not now take very seriously, it has been held to be necessary, at least in certain stages of the evolution of money, to give back to the giver-up of the something the full equivalent value in gold or other precious metal. If this equivalent were in the form of a certain weight of gold dust, or for that matter any other equally convenient exchangeable merchandise, we have merely a case of barter pure and simple, save only for the distinction that, in all probability, the recipient of the metal usually had no use for it himself and accepted it merely as a recognized temporary or intermediate form of payment. But when the practice of coining money arose, and coins were issued of definite weight and fineness stamped with some design, such as the king's head, indicative of the authority under which they were legalized as money, not only was a great step forward taken, as, for example, in convenience of reckoning without requiring the use of scales, but quite definitely the material of which the coin was made was thereby rendered useless to the owner, so long as the coin was not melted down. Within this limitation, that is so long as the coin remains intact, this type of money no less than modern credit or debt money, involved the giving up of something really for nothing, unless a miser's pleasure in gloating over his hoard be considered an economic value. Also it was quite customary to make it as treasonable an offence to deface the ruler's effigy or otherwise interfere with the intactness of a coin as to utter a counterfeit imitation. Though this may have been intended to prevent clipping, sweating, and the like, it gave the force of law to what is here taken to be the common essential criterion of all money, the voluntary forgoing of something of use or value to the owner *without* any equivalent return.

Paper Money

In the case of a paper note, it is still exactly what it was when it originated, a printed receipt for something given up for nothing. In the case of the original British banknotes it was at once the receipt of the bank issuing it for the equivalent of gold, voluntarily given up by the owner on loan or for safe keeping, and its promise to repay it on demand. Hence the origin of the legend *Promise to Pay* on our present notes. In their use as money the gold coin and paper note are on a par, the only difference being that the latter has no other possible function, whereas the former by being destroyed as money can revert to effective use as a commodity. We are here approaching two different considerations which are often confused, one, what gives money a definite exchange value, and the other, how that exchange value may be kept from changing, and how the owner may be safeguarded from loss should it be debased in value.

A gold or silver currency of full value is protected from being debased in value because it can be melted down, whether legally or not, and the bullion bartered for value equivalent to that given up for the money in the first place. Whereas any "unbacked" paper money is essentially a receipt merely or I.O.U. and, if it is debased in exchange value, the owner has no redress. It has been habitual for the professional money interests persistently to denigrate paper money, to keep alive the memory of every misuse of the printing press (which after all does give a tangible receipt to the owner for what he has given up), and to preach the virtues of gold whilst practising themselves an alchemy that did not even require the printing press. But to an unbiassed judge nothing could possibly be as bad as the system which grew up and flourished after it became physically impossible to increase the supply of gold sufficiently rapidly to keep pace with the expansion of industry, so that a substitute for it as money had to be found.

"Bank-Credit"

The ruinous continuous fall in price-level, so familiar today, is derived in the normal way from the checks imposed on the natural expansion of currency, required to keep pace with the increase of wealth in an era of expanding prosperity. The semblance of gold was preserved, but the system was really a gilded fraud. There grew out of a miserable 'backing' of gold (at first with, but ultimately without, the aid of any paper, or the issue of any receipt at all to the owner for what he had given up) a vast superstructure of physically non-existing money created by 'bank-credit We may postpone the nearer consideration of the technique till later. If printed receipts to the owners had been issued, the issue would have put into the shade the worst pre-War historical examples of the abuse of the printing press in times of political unrest and difficulty. It is not the issue of proper receipts that ought to be attacked, but the getting for nothing by the issue of money of more than the public are able to give up for it. If printing receipts, instead of giving gold for what the owner of money gives up for money, is an immoral practice, how much more immoral it is not even to give receipts! How utterly hypocritical it is to proceed against the counterfeiter of a forged note, who gives a false receipt, for treason rather than theft, and strictly to limit by Act of Parliament the amounts which the banks are allowed to obtain from the public for nothing by the issue of tangible receipts, while allowing them to extract for their own profit incomparable vaster amounts so long as they do not acknowledge the receipt at all!

The Private Issue of Money

By allowing private mints to spring up Parliament has fundamentally and perhaps irretrievably betrayed democracy. Before the war shed a penetrating light into the nature of money systems in general it was customary even in the works of apparently respectable economists to find absolutely dishonest hair-splitting distinctions between the invisible money so created and paper notes. The latter were really money and the former was not! In fact, the reader can always tell in such standard works on the subject when he is approaching the fishy part of the business. The essential fact, the creation of new money, becomes obscured in a cloud of anticipatory justification and elaborate special pleading. This is no longer even possible, and one may be thankful to find nowadays some technical writers on this malodorous subject who are content to state the facts unequivocally and to leave the reader to draw his own conclusion.

True, the old credit system "based on gold" kept the currency from being progressively and permanently debased relatively to the exchange value of gold by forcibly bringing it back again after it had been debased – by compounding for the robbing of Peter to pay Paul by the subsequent ruination of Paul to pay the bank. Simple, and in many ways good, as real gold and silver currencies are, they involve a vast amount of futile human effort in the search for the precious metals, which are then instantly rendered unavailing for any legitimate aesthetic or industrial application. But it is mere pretence to ascribe such solid advantages, as they may have, to modern systems pretending to be based on them, but really using them brutally to restore the value to money after it has been diluted, to the hurt of the innocent and profit of the guilty.

For over a century there simply has not been nearly enough gold and silver in the world for the requirements of a pure barter-currency. As regards actual present conditions in this country and elsewhere, since the final breakdown of the 'goldstandard', we are now committed to an almost pure credit-debt money, but instead of any definite standard we have entered upon a stage of 'monetary policy' in which the price-level is modified deliberately from time to time by irresponsible judges according to what they conceive to be 'policy', and without the slightest regard to the elementary principles of justice and fair dealing to those who own money, and that is to everyone in common, who have given up equivalent value for it.

Monetary Policy

Monetary policy would be better described as 'weights and measures policy', for it is simply a universal means of juggling with the standards of weight and measurement. No one outside of metrical science is really interested in the absolute value of the latter. The economic use of them is purely relative to money – how many pounds of coal to the £, how many pence for a pint of beer. Making the £ buy less or more of pounds or pints is the same in all economic affairs as making the pound and the pint weigh and measure less or more than before. It substitutes for false scales and measuring vessels universal and inescapable swindling mechanism.

We are living in an age rendered great by the precise sciences and it is idle to try and link our money still to the old semi-idolatrous lure of gold and silver. Books could be and have been written for and against the system of linking the exchange value of commodities to the one commodity, gold, without even attempting to answer the real question of what it is that does give money its exchange value. It is true that simple barter-currencies can keep money constant in value relatively to gold or silver. But that by itself has no meaning, unless an answer can be found for the question, what fixes the value of these relatively rare metals, almost completely confined in use to luxury purposes, in terms of the things universally necessary for life to continue at all? That there is a question to be answered is obvious when we deal with pure paper and credit forms of money, and it is almost as obvious that the answer can only be found in what is here taken as the essential feature of money in general, since it is the only feature this form of money exhibits. One has to give up just as much for a paper £1 as for a golden sovereign. There is no difference in the two kinds of money in this aspect, and so it is this aspect which is the common criterion of all forms of money.

What Gives Value to Money

Its exchange value depends, in fact, simply on the amount of wealth people voluntarily prefer to go without rather than to possess. The value of money depends to be sure on how much people want money, but the prevailing loose and confusing meaning attaching to any such phrase as 'people wanting money' makes it necessary to add "*instead* of wealth" Again, 'demand for money,' 'abundance or scarcity of money,' 'price of money,' and so on, are technical expressions of the loan market. In genuine loan transactions of any kind the lender *gives up* the credit that is money to another who expends it in his stead, and in national economics it is not the individual who spends it but the fact of it being spent that is of importance. Since people do not borrow money and pay interest on it merely to hoard it, genuine lending and spending in this connection are synonymous. Whereas what determines the value of money is the amount of wealth people prefer to go without; and that is the same as the amount of credit they *retain* as money.

All the common phraseology of money stresses only the something you get for it by getting rid of it, rather than the prior consideration of what you give up by acquiring and retaining it. From the first standpoint peoples' demands for it are insatiable; from the second it would be truer to say, misers excepted, that people keep as little of it as is safe. They want as much on the average as will enable them to conduct their avocations and domestic affairs without inconvenience and embarrassment. They want enough to buy what they can afford to buy as they need it. If they have more than this they spend or invest it. In either case they put on somebody else the onus of going without the things it will buy. It is highly important to recognize at once that investing is in this connection spending just as much as lending is and for the same reason. The reader must remember that in this inquiry the ordinary attitude of the individual to money is assumed to be perfectly understood, and it is not this aspect but rather the communal aspect of money that is being investigated.

Two Fundamental Monetary Principles

There are two considerations here that are of importance. The first is that buying, selling, investing, genuine lending, and borrowing, have no effect whatever on the quantity of money – and that is the quantity of wealth the community goes without – since what one person gets or gives up another gives up or gets. Somebody, that is to say, has to own all of the money all of the time, and go without the substance for the shadow. Much as individuals may appear to be free to exercise their choice, they are free only in so far as the requirements of others may be the opposite or complement of their own. If, among the community, buying is more in evidence than selling, the price-level rises and the value of the money unit falls. If selling predominates over buying, the opposite occurs. Assuming that the quantity of money does not change, the first means that the community chooses to give up less goods and service than when the price-level does not change; and the second that it chooses to give up more.

The second point of importance is that, though individuals die and their affairs are wound up, communities go on indefinitely. So that in a money system we are really not contemplating any temporary voluntary forgoing of something for nothing to suit the individual's preferences and convenience, but, on the part of the community, an enforced abstinence from use and ownership of buyable goods and services equal in aggregate price or value to the aggregate quantity of money in the community.

Virtual Wealth

This aggregate of exchangeable goods and services which the community continuously and permanently goes without (though *individual* money owners can instantly demand and obtain it from other individuals) the author terms the Virtual Wealth of the community. It fixes the value of the aggregate of money whatever the latter may be. The value of each unity of money, such as the £, in goods, or what is termed the "price-index" or "pricelevel", is thus the Virtual Wealth divided by the total aggregate of money. The latter in a credit-money system may be anything whatever, but the former is definite and is dictated by the necessity of people retaining sufficient instantaneously exercisable credit for goods and services to enable them to get what they want as they want it. They may have a great variety of Other forms of credit – goods, services, jewellery, investments, real estate, and property – but in a monetary civilization, as distinct from one practising barter, these all have first to be sold to a buyer, that is exchanged for the credit that is money, before people can get what they want as they want it. In this, selling services for money is, of course, more usually termed earning (wages, salary, fees, commissions, and so on).

The Community's Credit

What is here called by the special name *Virtual Wealth* is often intended by monetary reformers when the much wider and more general term, credit of the public or of the nation, is employed. In reality Virtual Wealth is a special and peculiar part of the credit of the nation. The credit of a nation may be, and for the most part is, in no way different from that of individuals, in the ordinary sense of their ability to run into debt. Thus the relation that governs the ordinary national debt is the same as if it were owed amongst individuals. The nation has drawn on or expended its credit to the extent of seven or eight thousand million pounds by borrowing these sums from individual citizens on various terms as regards interest payments and repayment, if ever, in the future, and these individuals own debts for the sums of money which they have empowered the Government to spend in their stead. They hand over their money and the Government buys itself goods and services.

The Virtual Wealth, on the other hand, is the credit established by individuals with the nation, through which, in the first place, the intermediate form of payment, money, comes into existence. It is established by goods and services being handed over directly to the issuer of money, repayable as such not from the issuer (unless issued by the nation) but from the community on demand, the debt not bearing interest to the creditor, so long as he retains the credit and right of instant repayment. Interest, obviously, can be exacted from debts only repayable, if at all, on some future date, and not on those which the owner can be repaid at any time but chooses to postpone payment.

Credit Money a Tax

But, from the standpoint of the community, credit money is simply a form of forced levy or tax impossible to resist, the aggregate of such creditors having no option in the matter, as in other forms of the debt-credit relation. Anyone issuing money, whether the State, bank, or counterfeiter, makes a forced levy on the goods and services of the nation which the existing creditors, in their capacity as money-owners, give up through the corresponding reduction in the value of each unit of their money. When taxation, or other form of expropriation of the property of the individuals by the State, has yielded all that the latter can be compelled to surrender, the last resort of the tax-gatherer – and it is completely inescapable – is the issue of new money, and it can be continued until the whole of the money is reduced to relative worthlessness. In this way, of course, after the war the defeated nations, Russia, Germany, and Austria, raised revenue when no other means were possible, and at the same time repudiated all pre-existing debts so far as they were repayable in money.

Many, no doubt, until they get familiar with it, will question the use or necessity of this conception of Virtual Wealth, and hold that it does not really explain the value of money. To individuals it may seem a quaint and sophisticated inversion of common usage. Rather it is the first step towards reversing the inversion induced in peoples' habits of thought by regarding money as the primary definite and important factor, and the wealth it will buy as a consequence or inherent property of money. It is the wealth all people must involuntarily give up and go without that is the primary factor that endows money with the power of buying at all. If all refused to go without anything for money and claimed all the wealth to which they are legally entitled in exchange for it, there would only be buyers but no sellers, and no wealth whatever to satisfy even a single one of them. In so far as the money may incorporate or be "backed" by a valuable material, which can be recovered by destroying it as money, there is this much to satisfy them, but in so far as it is pure credit money there is absolutely nothing.

"Backed" Money

If we consider an intermediate form such as a paper money "backed" by a deposit of some type of legal securities, then behind the one kind of debt, money, there is another kind of debt which the existing owner may be legally compelled to surrender. This may than be exchangeable for the wealth the owner needs much in the same way as, but less simply than, by money. But in this case it would still be true to say that the wealth which the owner of money has given up, and is owed for, does not exist. For the securities "behind" this sort of money are already in the, possession of owners, and the process is merely the enforced expropriation of their property in recovery of a repudiated debt. In Ruskin's words it is "the root and rule of all economy that what one person has another cannot have", and the worst blunders of the ordinary conventional economist will be found to have arisen from the attempt somehow to count twice over property with two owners, where, as in this case, the rights of the one begin only when those of the other end.

Money a Claim to What Does not Exist

The essential feature of money is, as McLeod fully understood, that it is a legal claim to wealth *over and above* the wealth in existence, all of which in an individualistic society is *already* in the ownership of others independently of this claim. Even in the case of a gold coinage bearing the imprint of the nation or its ruler it is quite customary and nearer the truth to regard the gold as the property of the nation or ruler rather than of the individual owner of the coin. So that, without any real exception, we reach the conclusion that over and above all the existing property, all of which has owners already, the owners of money possess claims to what they have given up, but what they have given up does not actually exist. The best physical analogy to this is to regard the wealth of a community as reckoned not from the zero of "no wealth", but from a negative datum line below it by the amount of the Virtual Wealth, just as for purposes of special surveys it may be convenient to reckon the level not from average sea-level as customary, but from some level below it, as, for instance, the lowest tidal-level. There is no real mystery about money, as there is about psychic phenomena, but merely a sort of spurious mathematical mysticism introduced by the invention for the purpose of calculation of imaginary negative quantities which are quite legitimate if the nature of the convention is understood. Unfortunately it is not.

The Price-Level

For all practical purposes the Virtual Wealth at every instant is "measured" (*in money value!*) by the aggregate of money. If the latter is a thousand millions the community are voluntarily refraining from possessing a thousand millions' worth of property which they have the right to own and do not. Nowadays the quantity of money does not stay put. It is varying wildly from minute to minute of the working day. From one year to another it may be arbitrarily varied within the year by hundreds of millions to suit some "policy" designed to increase or decrease the value of the unit. It is not, however, the Virtual Wealth that changes, that is a very conservative quantity indeed, as it is dictated by the people's necessities and habits, which they alone can change. But the Virtual Wealth being always divided up into a larger or smaller number of units, the price-level or value of each unit varies proportionally with the aggregate of money, considered as one independently operating factor. On the other hand, normally in these days of continuous expansion, over long enough periods there is and should be a steady gradual appreciation in the value of the Virtual Wealth, both on account of increase of population and on account of the rise of the standards of living. If this is not kept pace with under a credit-money system by the issue of correspondingly more money, we have the paralysis brought on by a continuously falling price-level and the ruination of producers in the interest of the rentier.

But, as will appear later, it is absolutely essential for the purpose that it should be issued freely as a gift to the nation, which gives up gratuitously the goods and services it is worth, and then only *after* the increase of prosperity has occurred when goods without money to buy them are actually awaiting sale. If, as in the past, it is issued as a debt to the banks for producers to buy goods and services to sink in new production, in addition to making the issuer of money the uncrowned king, it cannot be issued without raising the price-level. The general commonsense proof of the latter consequence is that you do not by mere tricks of accountancy, involving imaginary negative quantities, affect by one iota the physical processes by which new wealth is created, but only those by which the incidence of the distribution of the existing wealth among its various claimants and owners is effected. It is amazing, but nevertheless quite in keeping with the age that is passing away, that till quite recently it was common to ascribe to "the moral mystery of credit" and the peculiar virtues of the British banking system the expansion of wealth that was due to the growth of knowledge. Thus the "orthodox" fell into the very same error that they were, and are, so fond of ascribing to other, especially monetary, reformers, namely the absurdity of thinking that all could get rich by means of the printing press and by "tinkering with the currency".

Money from the Issuer's Standpoint

So far we have been dealing with money as a public instrument replacing barter and have traced the essence of the invention to its enabling those, with goods and services to dispose of, to give them up freely for nothing with a more or less certain assurance that, and as a *quid pro quo*, they thereby became empowered in turn to receive goods and services on the same terms from others as they need them. Now we have to look at the money from the point of view of those who have hitherto expounded it, to whom money is the *something* for *nothing* before anyone can get *anything*, as it is to those who issue it in the first instance. To these fortunate people the criterion as to what is and what is not really money appeared to depend on fine degrees of general acceptability. Usually an imaginary line was drawn between the banknote and the cheque on the ground that though both were in reality demands on the bank for money (which in this country is now no longer even true of the first), yet the bank-note had by custom become generally acceptable, whoever presented it, while the cheque was so only if tendered by the person to whom it was drawn or other person authorized by him.

All of this, from the standpoint of the public who use money for its legitimate purpose and spend the greater part of their lives striving that they may not be left without it, is pure sophistry, while on the academic side the analysis is entirely superficial. Since the war, it is refreshing to notice that even the orthodox admit, however much may be said for regarding the cheque as not really money, that there can be no dispute that the deposits at the bank on which the cheque is drawable, and which have come into existence as the result of the invention of the cheque system, are most certainly money. Thanks, no doubt, in part to the existence of monetary reformers and the ridicule they have poured on these shibboleths which are or were the stock-intrade of their opponents, but, even more, to the almost incredible blunders and confusions perpetrated since the war in the name of "sound finance", the general public is today too wide awake to the diametrically opposite interests of those who live by creating and destroying money, and of those

who have to acquire it as a licence to live at all, to be
hoodwinked any longer by such evasions.

Money not now a Tangible Token

The distinction between what has a physical and tangible
existence, like coins and notes, and what has not, like bank
deposits, is a highly sinister and dangerous one, but it is not
a distinction between what is money and what is not. A
legal right of action against a bank to supply money on
demand is to the owner of it as effective as money itself and
usually more convenient. It is of no great significance that
the bank is able to cancel, by the cheque system, the bulk of
the cheques drawn on it against those paid into it, so as to
dispense with tangible money altogether except for the
difference between the two amounts. This merely
substitutes for an automatic system of accounting by
physical counters a clerical book-keeping system which is
fraudulent because it does not start reckoning from zero but
from some *continuously varying* negative value.

Money is a right of action against the community to supply
goods and services or, what is the same thing, to discharge
the debt incurred through obtaining them from the vendor,
so that a right of action against a bank to supply money on
demand is a right of action *against the community* to supply
goods and services on demand. Every ordinary person, of
course, knows that money is a claim to goods and it is of no
practical importance if, in theory, he has to claim that claim
from a bank before he can claim the goods. One might as
lief argue that a bicycle left in a cloakroom was not a
bicycle but a right of action against the railway company to
supply a bicycle. The highly sinister and dangerous

distinction refers not to the aspect usually stressed, nor to that so far stressed in this chapter, but rather to the origin of the money and, if it is destroyed, to its destruction.

The definition of modern money with which we started makes clear that before it can come into existence some one has to give up something for nothing to the issuer of it in the first instance, and the aggregate the community so gives up is called the Virtual Wealth of the community. Dealing with a gold or silver money of full value the issuer has also to give up full value for the money, but he renders it, while used as money, merely a token otherwise useless, with the result that all the effort expended in the winning of the precious metals used as money is effectually wasted. But in the issue of every other form of money the issuer must get the something gratis.

Change-over from Barter to Credit-Money

It is easy to see this if we suppose a community practising barter or using a pure barter gold currency to change suddenly to a credit system. It would be similar to starting to play a game with money with a common pool, in which each of the players before he was entitled to play had to contribute so much money to the pool, except that, instead of money, in the one case goods or other exchangeable property and in the other case gold coins, now withdrawn and reverting to their original function as a commodity, would be paid into the pool in return for receipts in the form of the new credit-debt money. The consequence would be that the croupier, or authority in charge of the pool, would be holding in trust for the community various forms of property equal to the Virtual Wealth of the community. But as there is no intention of ever winding up the monetary system in the future, it is clear that all this actual wealth, equal to the Virtual Wealth in value, would remain permanently in the pool. If the community prosper and expand, the pool will naturally tend to grow rather than decrease, through the people increasing their Virtual Wealth and giving up the equivalent actual wealth for it in exchange for the receipts that are money. It can only decrease through the community decreasing in numbers or well-being and it can only be reduced to nothing by the community ceasing to exist.

There would then arise the situation which the banking profession first discovered and kept as a trade secret. They acted as croupiers and received the public's gold voluntarily surrendered to them on loan or for safe-deposit, and issued notes for it that were at once receipts for the gold given up and promises to pay it back on demand. Then these notes began to circulate as money. At first for every note that remained in circulation the gold lay idle in their safes, and on the average they always held a much larger quantity of gold than sufficed to repay those who, instead of using the notes to pay their debts, demanded the gold back from the bank. This did not last long, for, naturally, they began lending some of the gold out at interest to safe borrowers, and only kept enough to satisfy their clients demanding gold. The situation then was that they owed their depositors more gold than they could at any time repay, but were in turn owed as much gold by those to whom they *had* lent it, and were under bond to bring it back at some date in the future. But this did not last long either.

The False Step

It is this next step which ushers in money in its present modern sense in which it is an essentially new invention, and all the subsequent steps are merely elaborations of the original. For the bankers began soon to lend not gold but their own notes, or promises to repay gold which neither they nor their depositors possessed. Even if there was so much gold in existence at all, it was the property of and in the possession of others entirely outside the circle of their business. The situation, then, was, assuming that they only lent notes and no gold, keeping the latter as a "backing" for their note issue, that they owed gold to the extent of their client's "deposits" plus the outstanding note-issue in circulation, which they were pledged to redeem in gold if returned to them, and against the debt they held the gold backing in their vaults and the securities or "collateral" of their borrowers, that is of those to whom they had lent notes (promises to pay gold), but from whom, naturally, they would have to accept their own notes in repayment of the debt if presented to them instead of gold.

This is the origin of modern money as nothing for something on the part of the legitimate user; as something for nothing on the part of the issuer; and as something for a promise to pay it back on the part of the borrower, with sufficient security to whom the issuer transferred the acquisition of the something accruing *gratis* from the issue. It is all very easy to understand from the standpoint of Virtual Wealth, and the necessity that the aggregate of the individuals of the community must give up for nothing and be permanently owed for part of their possessions if they are to avoid barter or a barter-currency. If from the first the creation of money had been preserved, as it should have been, as the prerogative of the State, the chequered history of the last two centuries and the impending dissociation of the whole Western civilization would never have occurred. But the banker alone knew this aspect of money, and for long he kept it as the high secret of his trade. But it is a secret no longer.

Why was it False?

Why is it so vital to the safety of the realm that money, and particularly credit money, should be the prerogative of the Crown, as a central authority representing the whole nation? The reasons are numerous, but by far the most fundamental is apparent if we consider again the above stage, which represents the invention of modern money in the sense defined. A new currency has been created by the banks through people engaged in industry incurring debts to the banks *which cannot be repaid except by destroying that currency*, for there is nothing else to repay it with. When the banks borrowers have to repay they must either find gold, which for all the bankers knew or cared had no physical existence, or the bankers' own notes. Now these notes were not given away. The amount of the issue is the amount owed to the bank. By the issue of new money the debt to the bank is created and by the repayment of that debt the money is destroyed again. Clearly long before any great proportion could be repaid there must arise a shortage of money and all the remaining debtors would be physically unable to obtain the money, that is to sell their produce or manufactures at any price.

The Banker as Ruler

From that invention dates the modern era of the banker as ruler. The whole world after that was his for the taking. By the work of pure scientists the laws of conservation of matter and energy were established, and new ways of life created which depended upon the contemptuous denial of such primitive and puerile aspirations as perpetual motion and the ability ever really to get something for nothing. The whole marvellous civilization that has sprung from that physical basis has been handed over, lock, stock, and barrel, to those who could not give and have not given the world as much as a bun without first robbing somebody else of it. Industry and agriculture, the producers of the positive wealth by virtue of which communities live, can only expand by getting deeper and deeper into debt to the banks. They have been reduced to permanent and inescapable bondage by a subtle and, in its place, useful form of accountancy that continues to count below the level at which there is anything to count. The skilled creators of wealth are now become hewers of wood and drawers of water to the creators of debt, who have been doing in secret exactly what they have condemned in public as unsound and immoral finance and have always refused to allow Governments and nations to do openly and above board. This without exaggeration is the most gargantuan farce that history has ever staged.

The Profits of the Issue of Money

We left our hypothetical community suddenly changing from barter to credit-debt money, with the central issuing authority in possession of gold and other property of value equal to the Virtual Wealth of the community, and the latter in possession instead of the receipts for what they had given up which are to serve them in future for ever after as money. Clearly the whole stock of valuable property in the possession of the issuer cannot in practice be left as a "backing" for the money. All of it if unused, except the gold and jewels, would rot. As there is not enough of such imperishable forms of wealth to serve as money, it is idle to relegate all there is to the utter waste of permanent incarceration in strong rooms and vaults, as part security for a debt that can never be repaid except by the community reverting to the primitive barter system which it has outgrown. It needs but common sense to suggest that it should all be used at once for the general purposes of the community by defraying part of the necessary public expenditure out of this store, which would otherwise have to be met by taxation. As the Virtual Wealth of the community grows, the further wealth it has to give up for the further new money it needs ought also to be devoted to the same purpose.

Many people commencing the study of money over-estimate the amounts that can be got from the community for nothing by its issue. It is even suggested that taxation could be entirely met this way and still some would be left over for free distribution! But the amounts so obtainable *gratis* are not likely to embarrass any modern Government! Though large from the point of view of the individual, they are small compared with the scale of national expenditure. Lively hopes again have been entertained in many quarters of providing national dividends out of such new money, but these seem to depend on simple mistakes as to the nature of an actual, or, indeed, conceivable, money system. Any given single quantity of money will normally go on distributing goods and services *for ever* at a constant rate if the price-level remains unchanged, so that the total quantity of goods and services it will forward from production to consumption and use is unlimited. No new money at all can be issued unless and until there is an increase of the rate of production. It is only when *the rate* of production and consumption increases, that is to say when the quantities of wealth produced and consumed per year, or in any other unit of time, increase, that proportionally more money has to be issued if the price-level is to remain the same.

Money Indestructible without Expropriation

It is nonsense to suppose it can be destroyed "when it has done its work". It cannot be so destroyed without the owner of it being expropriated of his claim to goods and services. The facility with which the banks can destroy money as well as create it depends on the fact that such money is not given away at all, but only lent, and the credit money that was created for the borrower is automatically expropriated from him again and disappears from existence when he repays the loan. Whereas the suggestion to pay national dividends out of such credits does not contemplate lending money at all but giving it away, and such claims to wealth cannot be destroyed again except by taxation, or some other form of expropriation, compelling the owner to surrender up for destruction the money so issued. It is positively amazing how ready some people are to believe in magic still.

It is not, of course, contended that the profits of the issue of new money could not be issued to consumers as a national dividend, but merely that the amounts would hardly be worth while, since practically every consumer already pays far more in taxes than he could hope to receive from such a source. It would seem more natural to use the profits of the issue of new credit money for the general relief of the taxpayer. But the total quantities of money that have been privately issued in the past would, if now applied to the relief of the taxpayer, effect a very worth-while reduction in his burden, something like £2 per head of population per year. Once this were done the further annual amounts that would be necessary in this country, if distributed, either as a relief to taxpayers or as a national dividend, could hardly be more than a few shillings per head per annum, that is if the price-level is not to be increased. If the price-level is not held constant, but allowed to rise continuously until ultimately the money becomes worthless, then, of course, there is no limit at all ta the amount of money that can be distributed as a national dividend, or issued in lieu of imposing taxation. But to contend that a worth-while national dividend can be issued and prices prevented from rising by legal enactments is nowadays absurd. For everything so got *gratis* must be exactly accounted for in the new economics by others going without it, that is by their *retaining* without spending it more money than before by the extra amount issued. They must do this anyway, but whether that means that they are voluntarily giving up more wealth for it than before is entirely a question of the price-level. If they cannot afford to do so then the price-level will rise and the money becomes worth less.

CHAPTER III

THE EVOLUTION OF
MODERN MONEY

THE Origin of the Cheque

In point of time the invention of the cheque antedates that of the bank-note, originally a promise to pay gold on demand. It was customary for merchants who had deposited gold for safe keeping at the goldsmiths, the originators of "banking" as it is still called, to write an order or instruction to them to hand over some definite amount of their gold to another person than themselves, named in the order, who, on presenting it and endorsing it as evidence that it had been carried out, was paid this amount. It was a means of settling accounts with creditors by instructing the keeper of the debtors' funds to settle them without the debtors needing themselves to draw out the money, which is exactly analogous to the modern cheque.

From the first, however, the bankers developed the bank-note, for this was a powerful means of spreading their reputation for honest dealing and trustworthiness through the whole community. People finding they could always if they wished exchange bank-notes at the bank for gold, became accustomed to accept them whoever tendered them in payment, and not to change them for gold at the bank except for special reasons, as when going abroad, whereas the name of the drawer of a cheque would be known to relatively few people and therefore had not the same degree of general acceptability as the note as a form of money. Honest dealing and trustworthiness then meant ability to give the gold for the paper whenever asked. At that time it was what mattered most, and there is no doubt that the early banker was a social benefactor in inventing a credit medium of exchange when gold no longer sufficed. This old-fashioned type of banker would be appalled at the terrible power that he has placed in less scrupulous hands.

It was to the banks' direct interest to see that counterfeit imitations of their notes were promptly detected and removed from circulation, and that those issuing them were tracked down and severely punished for doing, as it now appears, something far less socially dangerous in its ultimate consequences than what the bankers were doing themselves. But at that stage in the evolution of money the physical impossibility of repaying the debts they were so careful to create for that purpose was not understood, and the public were still firmly convinced that the convertibility of the paper into its nominal worth of precious metal constituted the note money. Whereas the paper itself was money because the owner had given up that value of goods and services to acquire it, and was therefore entitled to an equivalent value in exchange for it. The whole money-issuing interests, however, continued by every means in their rapidly growing power sedulously to propagate the other point of view. That is why they and the politicians thought that there would be an outcry when there came into force at the outbreak of the war the scheme for recalling all the gold and substituting a pure credit money. But there was no outcry whatever, most people actually preferring in use the new paper notes to golden sovereigns. Neither has there been any justification, from the point of view of public prejudice, for the persistent and ruinously unsuccessful post-War efforts to return to gold. What the public want is a constant price-index, so that the value of money remains stable in goods and services. That they cannot have, as we shall see, without destroying "banking" as now understood. Here, as always, one has to distinguish very sharply between the interests of the public and those of their real rulers; and so far democracy has never had a government that could trust itself to rule independently of the money-power.

Government Regulation of "Banking"

But though the public were sedulously protected in the banks' interest from the counterfeiter, they were not protected from the failures of the banks to redeem their impossible promises, which became so frequent and caused such widespread ruin that the whole monetary system in this stage of transition was jeopardized. There were many reasons for this. The Government having allowed in the first instance the banks to usurp their prerogative in creating money, instead of creating it themselves, attempted in every possible way to hamper and thwart them. So far, at least, as the country and commercial banks were concerned, they were suspicious and hostile to innovations which seemed to go against the ordinary standard of commercial morality and to be a new form of counterfeiting. But as regards themselves they acted differently. Instead of issuing sufficient money themselves, they more and more favoured and empowered one bank, the Bank of England, to act for them in return for its raising revenue for Government purposes. This bank was founded in 1694 in the reign of William III, on the model of earlier Italian banks, to provide the Government with funds, and it lent money at interest first in return for permission to issue notes of equal amount, and was soon rewarded by a monopoly of note issue, redeemable in gold coin on demand, which lasted till 1709. From its genesis to this day it has never been a bank of the English nation, but a bank to provide the Government with money primarily and principally for war expenditure – a weapon which the Government can, and does, employ against the people. But from being what is known as a bankers' bank, it has become now almost the Government's government.

Outside of this object State regulation of "banking" has been restrictive. Speciously directed to protecting the public from being swindled by dishonest and unsubstantial banks, it rendered the position of honest and then socially minded bankers so precarious that their failure and the consequent ruination of merchants and commercial people became almost inevitable. The policy culminated in the Bank Charter Act of Sir Robert Peel of 1844, which nominally fixed the monetary system in this country up to the war, but through which the banks soon found they could drive a coach-and-four. It legislated to limit and ultimately to extinguish the issue of bank-notes in England except by the Bank of England, limiting the latter's issue to fourteen millions above the gold reserve (the so-called fiduciary issue, because it was supposed to be founded on the public's confidence rather than on their necessities). This effectively checked the expansion of the note currency and the upshot was that the cheque, at first secretly, took the place of the note as a means of creating new money and soon became the overwhelmingly preponderating form of the credit medium of exchange.

Lending Cheque-Books

Instead of printing and lending notes, an obvious creation of money, this much more insidious and dangerous form of issue grew up. The borrower without money was allowed to draw cheques just as if he had money and to create an overdraft at the bank. The bank's balance-sheet was falsified so that it still balanced. For on the one side would be credited to the individual the limiting sum up to which he was authorized to overdraw and on the other side the same sum as owing as a debt of the individual to the bank. Naturally, as always, substantial security or "collateral" had to be deposited with the bank before the privilege was granted, considerably more in value than the amount of the overdraft, to provide an ample margin of safety to the bank. If the debtor defaulted a forced sale of the security recovered from the public the sums he had been allowed by his overdraft to put into circulation. Under such circumstances the security could not be expected to fetch its real value. As, moreover, such liquidations occur in times of bankruptcy when money is scarce and prices low, whereas "loans" are wanted in times of boom when money is abundant and prices high, the banks so were enabled to acquire valuable securities at forced-sale prices. They had only to hold the securities till "confidence" returned, when they were re-issuing the money they had called back so that it was again plentiful, to realize much more for them than they had fetched when sold to recover from the public the money the overdraft had put into circulation. It is important to realize that whichever way it works it is a case for the bank of "Heads I win, tails you lose". Moreover, the money in which they are repaid is, on the average, worth more in goods than that which they create to lend.

There was essentially nothing new in this, or different in principle from lending "promises-to-pay-gold" instead of gold itself, save that the banks avoided the necessity of giving printed receipts for the goods and services their borrowers obtained for nothing, and there was a secret instead of open creation of money. Instead of lending notes, the banks, in effect, now lend chequebooks and the right to draw cheques up to limited sums beyond what the borrower possesses. For nearly a century, until the revelations of the war made it impossible to conceal the truth from the general public, the bankers stoutly denied that they were creating money at all, and claimed that they were merely lending the deposits their clients were not using. The President of the Bank of Montreal not a year ago continued to repeat this, but, nearer the centre of things, all this was known and admitted by the orthodox apologists for this monstrous system even before the war, usually by some such lying phrase as "Every loan makes a deposit".

Genuine and Fictitious Loans

For a loan, if it is a genuine loan, does *not* make a deposit, because what the borrower gets the lender gives up, and there is no increase in the quantity of money, but only an alteration in the identity of the individual owners of it. But if the lender gives up nothing at all what the borrower receives is a new issue of money and the quantity is proportionately increased. So elaborately has the real nature of this ridiculous proceeding been surrounded with confusion by some of the cleverest and most skilful advocates the world has ever known, that it still is something of a mystery to ordinary people, who hold their heads and confess they are "unable to understand finance It is not intended that they should. But if, instead of trying to puzzle it out along the lines of "what you get for money", these people will reverse the procedure, as in this book, and do so on the of "what you give up for it", the trick is clear enough.

Current Account Deposits

Cheque-account deposits at the bank represent, in monetary units of value, what the owners have given up in the way of goods and services in order to acquire these claims to equivalent goods and services on demand. In so far as one spends his money another receives it, or in so far as one receives the goods and services owing to him another gives them up and is credited for them. With true "time deposits", however, it is quite different, though banking practice has been directed to slurring over the distinction. In an honest money system this difference would be insisted upon as essential to accurate accountancy. However, this is too important a matter to deal with incidentally, and its consideration will be postponed. We will confine the argument here to cheque account deposits.

The aggregate of the cheque-accounts, exclusive of genuine time-deposits, represents in units of money value, as stated, what the owners of money (*not* the borrowers of it) dealing with the banks are owed on demand in goods and services from the nation in which the money is legal tender. These vast sums of money are entirely of the bank's creation in the first instance. When the bank pretends to lend their money they do not reduce the amount of the claims of the owners to goods and services on demand by a farthing. They do not inform them that they can no longer draw it out as it has been lent to others! They create among the general body of vendors who supply goods and services, in exchange for the cheques the banks authorize their borrowers to draw, *new* claims on the community for goods and services. When these cheques are paid into the vendors' accounts they create new deposits at the banks. When the borrowers repay their loans and balance their accounts, they withdraw money for the purpose from those to whom they sell goods and services, and by cancelling their overdrafts this money then disappears from existence, just as unaccountably as it made its appearance. If we can imagine the impossible, that they ever succeeded in freeing themselves from their indebtedness to the banks, every penny left would be worth half-a-crown and people earning £3 a week would get 2s. a week.

Why Cheque-money is Preferred to Tokens

We have only to substitute physical counters or receipts to show the utter dishonesty of the accounting. For if a man surrenders a physical money token, whether to lend it to somebody else or to buy something with it from somebody else, there's an end of it so far as he is concerned. He cannot ever lend or spend it again. He has to earn another or wait till his loan falls due before he can get another back to lend or spend again. But a man who deposits his money in a cheque account can lend or spend it exactly as though he had not deposited it at all, by using a cheque for the amount, and yet it is this same money the bank pretends it lends out.

The Gold-Standard

It is only necessary very briefly to consider the now obsolete methods by which, up to the war, the quantity of money in existence was kept in the perpetual state of ebb and flow known as the Trade Cycle or Credit Cycle, by making it convertible with gold. The details of this "beautifully working automatic regulation" is the stock-in-trade of all pre-War conventional money writers, and need not detain us. The quantity of money was regulated by means of the gold-standard. The latter meant that the value of the money unit in a large number of countries was kept equal to that of a certain weight of gold by making the money in theory always exchangeable with gold. In practice it meant the growth of a number of new devilries having for their object the frustration of every attempt to exchange it for gold, so soon as that exchange began to occur. Since there was only enough gold in the whole world to be had for a miserable fraction of the claims to gold, which the easy method of lending cheque-books had brought into existence, in no case must the bankers be caught out. Everyone else bore the losses. Boom or slump, the banker throve.

It was easy to fix the money price of gold, but what fixed the goods price of gold? Gold being given a fixed price, the price of every other commodity now varied in relation to the one arbitrarily fixed. The average price, or the pricelevel, during last century varied enormously. There were five well-marked periods of changing value in all countries, due to innumerable causes. Apart altogether from human and psychical influences, some of the more obvious physical ones were the discovery of gold mines, the invention of new technical processes by which gold is extracted, the number of countries having gold currencies in comparison with those having silver currencies, and so on. It was really much worse than standardizing the barometer height, calling it a "bar", whatever it was, and expressing all lengths in terms of what the "bar" happened to be at the moment. The variation of the pricelevel in terms of gold was, however, over a range of two or three to one. This makes the variation of the barometer height in terms of the yard or of the yard in terms of the barometer height, whichever be taken as the "standard", almost negligible by comparison.

The capacity of the banks to create money without giving up anything for it depended on their always having enough legal tender (convertible into gold) to meet the demands of their depositors; that is, of those who have deposited money on 'current account In practice it was found that about fifteen per cent of their total deposits sufficed for their safety but, as the use of cheques continually increases, the percentage falls. The factor of safety is now considered to be about ten per cent, but may not be nearly as much. Nobody but the bankers themselves can see, in an age of potential plenty, any sense in their always trying to make do the work of £10 or more, when they have actually created claims to nine others which the owners have only to ask for to reduce them to panic, and send them howling to the Government for a moratorium.

The Correct Procedure

The proper thing to do, of course, would be for the Government to issue as many pounds as the citizens have given up *gratis* pound's worth of goods and services, not one-tenth as many, and it should require the banks to hold for ever after £1 of national money for every £1 in the current accounts of the banks' depositors.

Since banking became in reality minting by issuing cheque-books instead of notes, the banks have never been solvent, but have been liable to have to stop payment so soon as they were asked for more than one-tenth of the money (legal tender) they owed to their current account depositors. The measure proposed above would make them solvent for the first time in the modern phase of their history. The money being always in the banks, there would be an end of the frenzied shipments of gold back and forth, to raise the value of money here and depress it there, to throw goods intended for export suddenly on to the home market and as suddenly to drain the home market and ship the goods abroad, and all the nefarious and unscrupulous devices which, in the course of a century's experience of this secret private minting, have been invented to keep the world poor and maintain the supply of hardworking borrowers in an age of plenty.

Outside of this real explanation, the sole ostensible reason of it all is to prevent people from asking for the money for which they have had to give up the equivalent value in goods and services, but for which the Government has hitherto omitted to issue proper receipts. True the Government has not done so because it has as yet not received the goods and services, but the hard-working borrowers have received the money and have moreover furnished ample security in the way of collateral for every pound they have borrowed. The proposal, therefore, is that the Government should issue the necessary money to the banks in exchange for the borrowers' collateral, so that henceforth these borrowers owe, not the banks, but the nation which, not the banks, has supplied the goods. They can then repay their debts without destroying the nation's currency and making it impossible for them to find the money to pay. For as the loans fall due and are repaid, the Government should put the money back into circulation (or into the pound-for-pound deposits of cheque users) by buying with it National Debt securities and destroying them. Thus an equivalent of interest-bearing National Debt would be destroyed for the non-interest bearing National Debt that *is* money. For this money *has* been secretly issued by the banks through the cheque system. This occurred when the Government stopped them from issuing bank-notes and sought to restrict and control this form of currency through the Bank of England. It is time the legality of these operations was tested in the Courts. It is a curious kind of law that makes the open issue of money treason and its secret issue under a camouflaged name, as bank-credit, so immune from penalty that it was, till recently, treason even to question its legality. But that is now all out-of-date.

The Credit or Trade Cycle

Up to the outbreak of the War the system worked out its inevitable cycle in a relatively simple manner something as follows.

I. A period in which the increase of money (through more bank loans on the average being issued than are repaid) occurs faster than the Virtual Wealth increases and prices are therefore rising. There is abundance of goods *in course* of production but owing to the loans being made when the production is initiated – rather than in the correct manner, the new money being issued to consumers, in relief of taxation, after the new production has matured and is ready to be sold – production and consumption are put out of phase. Production lags behind consumption by about half the average period of time taken to produce, since the new money takes out of the market finished wealth to pay the workers, and the latter only put in unfinished wealth at its initial or some intermediate stage. Later it will be necessary to revert to this fundamental physical fallacy of the bankers' whole monetary system.

But it is easy to see, even at this stage, both why prices must rise and why the Virtual Wealth cannot increase to the extent of the increase of money so that the value of the latter is maintained. People are always at the market with money to buy some months on the average before the goods are there. This causes a drain on the existing stocks, and shortage of finished wealth, so that unless prices rose there would be no goods at all to sell for that part of the whole money equal to the extra amount created. Of course prices rise so that this does not happen. But all get less goods for their money than before. The money now being worth less than before, people have to retain more of it to possess the same Virtual Wealth (or credit for goods and services) as before. Soon the increased quantity of money buys no more than the original quantity did.

2. Though all other prices are rising, that of gold is arbitrarily fixed. This, in itself, only means that gold falls in value relatively to goods. The effects of new issues of credit money are the same as if new gold mines had actually been discovered. The rise of prices tends to make existing gold mining unprofitable and mines unable to pay which before could do so, which again will reduce the output of gold. But any such influence as this, decreasing the *annual* production of gold, can only produce a minute difference in the aggregate quantity of gold, and could only produce a

perceptible effect on the price-level after a long time. The actual demand for gold, outside of a backing for credit money, is now not great. It is really rather a useless metal at its price. This change of ratio between the values of gold and goods in itself could produce no automatic regulating effect in a self-contained community, since gold hardly enters into the category of commodities most people buy in order to be able to live. But, of course, the rise of prices swindles all creditors for the benefit of debtors.

The effect of the gold-standard, however, is to make gold international money. Since money is a debt only on that community of which it is the legal tender for the settlement of debts, and not a debt in the least acknowledged by or enforceable against any other country whatever, international interindebtedness must be settled by the transfer of actual goods or services from the country owing to the country owed, in so far as it is not of the nature of, or is converted into, a permanent loan or investment, bearing interest. Making legal tender convertible into gold thus means that, when the prices of everything else have risen and that of gold has not, indebtedness to a country abroad is more cheaply settled by shipping gold rather than other goods. We have seen that the first stage results in a permanent shortage of goods, through production permanently lagging behind consumption. This naturally creates a demand for goods, and goods can now be bought abroad wherever they are cheap and plentiful and paid for by shipping gold in exchange, rather than other goods, since everything else but gold has risen in price. Prices are in terms of the depreciated currency in the home market but at the old rate abroad. Hence the gold stocks of the country are drained out in this second stage, and under the system existing before the war, when the public were entitled to ask for gold in exchange for notes and cheques, the ratio between "cash" and credit (total deposits) at the banks was reduced ultimately below the limit the banker considered essential to his solvency.

3. The banker now decreases the quantity of money in existence by not renewing his loans so fast as they are repaid. These loans, contracted in a period of rising prices, have now to be paid back in a period of falling prices so that, through the change in the purchasing power of money and quite apart from the interest paid for the loan, the goods and services that have to be given up by the borrowers to obtain the money to repay must always on the average be greater than those obtained by them with the money they were lent. Before any considerable proportion of these loans can be paid it becomes impossible to obtain the money, that is to sell goods, except at a ruinous loss to the producers. Hence a number of them are rendered bankrupt. Their collateral is sold by the bank, or, if it will not now fetch the amount to repay the loan, appropriated by them. In this connection those borrowers who have been most deserving, and whose assets are therefore worth more than those who have been less efficient and careful in the conduct of their businesses, are those first victimized. They are sold up and ruined when those whose assets would not meet the claims of the bank have a better chance to escape in the hope they may be more worth selling up later.

How the Losses are Distributed

Under (1) the money the banks create is paid for by the whole community by the loss of the purchasing power of the pre-existing money. All contracts for future periodic payments for services, such as wages, salaries, interest, and rents, and those fixed by law or custom, such as transport fares, postal services, and professional fees, are vitiated to the injury of those who receive money while those who receive these services obtain an uncovenanted benefit, exactly as if there had been a universal shrinkage in weight of the pound, the volume of the pint, or the length of the yard. This is the inflation period in the only sense the term has any meaning, namely the period when the worth of money suffers debasement.

Under (2) there is a profound international disturbance endangering the friendly relations between nations which we still have to go into at greater detail. Under (3) we have the deflationary period, when the value of money is being brought back to the value in gold it originally had. There is general economic paralysis through the efforts of the debtors to repay their debts destroying the means of payment. In the whole system the fundamental purpose of money has been lost sight of. Instead of being a means for enabling a community freely to forward goods and services from the producer to the ultimate consumer and user, the interests of the whole community have been sacrificed to enable banks to lend more money than exists in physical or tangible form. There is not the slightest reason why just as much should not so exist as the economics of the country require, so long as it is issued only when additional wealth is awaiting sale. The situation has arisen through the failure of the nation to exercise its prerogative over the issue of money and through the banks' preference for a method which avoids the issue of proper national receipts, or anything at all in return, to those who have given up goods and services for the money. Nor is there the slightest reason for the existence of banking at all as it has now become, whatever may have been the case two centuries ago. The public own the goods and services the banker indents upon without furnishing anything in return for the levy and they pay for the private issue of money by being deprived of the profits of the issue, as well as by the rise of prices the incorrect mode of issuing it entails.

Fraudulent Monetary Terminology

The whole terminology of the system is inverted. Thus bank-credit, when the accounting is done in goods and services rather than figures, should be bank-debt, the debt of the banks to the community for the goods and services the banks have levied upon the nation by empowering impecunious borrowers to obtain them without payment. Again in the all-important cash to credit ratio, which in different epochs has varied from fifteen per cent to probably as low as seven per cent or less, both terms are false. We may postpone the consideration of the second, which is simply *the sum* of the current account and time "deposits", and is really the debt of the bank to its depositors for money on demand *and* on due notice. It is the public's credit and the banks' debt. But as regards "cash", as the veriest tyro knows now, by far the greater part even of this "cash" is now created by the Bank of England, debts of the latter to the clearing house banks being accounted as "cash". We may postpone also the nearer consideration of this for later consideration. Under Government protection this bank seems to think it a great joke bamboozling the public.

The Gold Drain

The devices for tinkering with the currency and making a minimum of genuine national money the base for the support of, probably, a ten – to twentyfold greater inverted pyramid of the will-of-the-wisp magically appearing and disappearing money called "bank-credit", and the method of regulation of the total money in existence by the Bank of England, were of a brutal and utterly callous character. The drain of gold from the Bank of England under (2) "automatically" resulted in a reduction in the total quantity of money in existence ten to twenty times the amount of gold removed. For each shilling or two of gold money that left the country without replacement £1 was destroyed by the banks arbitrarily calling on their borrowers to repay their loans – as we have seen, an impossibility. The invention of a new currency, as a debt to the issuing bank which could never after be repaid, because repayment destroyed the currency and the means of payment, put the whole wealth-producing system of the world in pawn to the banker. Ever after the world was in his absolute power.

The evils of genuine usury in the Middle Ages, through the shortage of the precious metals and insufficiency of the medium of exchange, cried aloud to heaven for redress. But the genuine usurer did at least give up what he lent and that for which he received interest, whereas the banker does not, but levies upon the goods and services of the nation for what he pretends to lend and upon which he receives interest. It is bad enough to be put in the grip of the money-lender who does lend his money, but it is a million times worse to be in the grip of the pretended moneylender who does not lend his own money but creates it to lend and destroys the means of repayment just as fast as the debtors succeed in repaying it. This is a surrender of the powers of life and death over the nation's economic life into the hands of irresponsible impostors.

The Government's Connivance

That the Government have always been a party to this abrogation of their function was revealed in the clearest manner at the outbreak of the war, when, for the first time in history, the throttle-hold of the banks on industry suddenly relaxed, and the economic system was allowed to work all out on production for the purpose of war destruction. The engines of the money system were quietly reversed before the first shot had been fired. Nations engaged in a world struggle to the death with other nations cannot afford to remain paralysed in the spider's web of bank finance. Then the banks were instructed to lend without limit to finance the production of munitions, and the Government undertook to print and issue to them the well-known "Bradburies" or National Treasury Notes, in denominations of £1 and 10s., as required to preserve their solvency and the safe ten per cent cash to credit ratio, irrespective of the amount of credit they issued. The appalling rise of prices was of course attributed by all the City gramophones to the floods of paper money issued by the Government.

In this way, by the printing and issue of three or four hundred millions of Treasury Notes, the aggregate amount of money was increased from some £1,200 millions in 1914 to some £2,700 millions in 1920, being more than doubled. The value of £1 in goods fell to less than one-half of what it would buy before the war. The increase of the National Debt, due to the war, some £8,000 millions, was for the most part contracted in this debased money, and if the money had been correctly issued the debt *would not have amounted to half this sum.*

The Cunliffe Committee

But before the war was even ended, the necessary cunning steps had been taken to bind the nation in the spider's web of bank finance again. The notorious Cunliffe Committee was set up to advise on the nation's monetary system when peace was restored. It was composed, with the exception of one academic orthodox economist – like all the others of that day still entirely uncritical of the honesty of the banking profession – entirely of the bankers themselves, and of Treasury Officials working hand in glove with them. It is significant of the close relations between the Government and the banking profession that several Treasury officials have since left the Government to become bank directors, including the one whose name the public associated with the Treasury Note. The Committee contained not a single representative of the interests either of consumers or producers, for whose benefit, and not for the benefit of the banking profession or the Treasury, money really exists. Nor did it contain a single monetary reformer although, even then, Arthur Kitson had been exposing the evils of the nation's monetary system for over twenty years, and had correctly predicted the inevitable consequences of allowing the bankers to resume their control over it.

The first recommendation of this Committee was the early return to the gold-standard and, the second, that the National Treasury Notes should be retired and replaced by bank-notes. The intended effect of the first was well within the understanding of the ordinary stock-exchange dealer or estates steward, whose business it is to know about these matters in their clients' interests. It meant that the National Debt, the overwhelming proportion of which was contracted in a debased currency, should be repayable as regards principal and interest in gold money worth over twice as much. The French knew all about this, and it is idle to pretend the British experts did not. It was justified as "correcting" the war inflation, when all the nations' pre-War creditors had been swindled through the banks' pretending to lend, and not lending but creating, some fifteen hundred millions to finance production. This would never have occurred at all if the loans had been genuine loans, which at the outbreak of the war there would not have been the slightest difficulty in raising from the public. This wrong the Cunliffe Committee proposed to correct by a second and worse one, the universal swindling of debtors in turn for the benefit of the war-gorged creditors, since debts and the interest on them are not really paid in pounds but in the goods and service the pounds will buy. But all this is now common knowledge, and sordid beyond concealment.

Deflation

The Report of the Cunliffe Committee was adopted and the Coalition Government of 1920 started to put it into operation. The ruinous deflation stage, N^o. (3) of the cycle, plunged the whole nation into economic paralysis from which it has hardly yet shown any signs of recovering. Apart from the physical destruction and loss of life and health among the actual combatants during the war, and the financial losses suffered by the purely rentier class through the inflation, the country at the signing of peace was in a condition of economic prosperity and well-being through the temporary removal of the stranglehold of money.

The most absurd propaganda now began in the Press, the public being exhorted to produce more and consume less one week, and the next, to work short-time and share one's job with one's pal. The banks began suddenly to contract credits with the object of raising the value of the money and lowering prices, quite undeterred by the rising tide of bankruptcies and unemployment. But, though they found it easy enough to produce universal ruin and misery, to lower prices was not so easy, the country producing and consuming less and less at the old price with the smaller quantity of money in existence, rather than the same as before at correspondingly lower prices.

The main reason for this is that lowering of prices means corresponding lowering of wages and salaries, which is effectively resisted by Trades and Professional Unions. The weaker are driven to the wall and lose their employment, so that they become a charge on the taxpayer, while those that retain their employment correspondingly benefit by any lowering of prices that may be forced. In fact the brutal methods of the gold-standard were too hopelessly out-of-date to reduce the price-level effectively after the war. Its principles were then quite as well understood by the economic advisers of industrial employers and of Labour as by the financial hierarchy. Moreover, in an age of abundance such as science has inaugurated, it is no longer possible to use the naked weapon of starvation to reduce recalcitrant workers to a lower standard of living as it was a century ago. Nor is it possible to expect business men to engage in production when they are told that, before their product comes on the market, prices will have fallen below what the product costs to make!

The Return to Gold

But by 1925 it was considered that the deflation policy had succeeded in its object sufficiently to risk the gold-standard being restored, as regards the foreign exchanges. The Gold Standard Act, 1925, made it possible to buy whole bars of gold of some four hundred Troy ounces weight at the pre-War price of gold. This openly gave a bounty to importers of goods from abroad, inviting them to use our stock of gold, with which they were provided at far below its market price, to export in exchange for foreign goods to compete against those in the home market. The costs of home producers were of course incurred in the still depreciated internal currency, whereas those of the foreigners were paid in gold units of much superior purchasing power. It was probably a desperate last effort of the bankers to break down the resistance to their policy of lowering prices, by subjecting the home market to bounty-aided foreign competition, but it could not and did not last long.

True-Blue Treason

The second recommendation of the Cunliffe Committee was carried out by the 1928 Currency and Bank Notes Act of the last Conservative Government. This, as will appear, fundamental change of the British Constitution was not made in any way a political issue. The Government as the true-blue upholders of the King and Constitution quietly, and with the minimum of fuss, authorized the retiral of the National Treasury notes bearing the King's head and the substitution for them of banknotes bearing the Bank of England's Promise to Pay. At best this promise could have very little meaning, but it was rendered entirely bogus when the Coalition Government of 1931 went off the gold-standard! The decision to do this was all the more surprising inasmuch as the ostensible reason of the Coalition Government was to prevent such a "calamity" from overtaking the nation. That, at least, was the reason given during an election campaign based even less on truth and reality than is now customary.

The 1928 Act

The 1928 Act, "deeming" the Treasury Notes to be bank-notes, made provision for their replacement by a "fiduciary" issue of £,260 millions of Bank of England Notes above the gold reserve, with provision for the increase or decrease of this issue by consultation between the Bank and the Treasury, it being subsequently increased by 15 millions when the gold-standard was abandoned in 1931. Much is said in this Act about the purely nominal liability of the Bank for this issue and little about the profits of the issue, but it seems clear that the net profits, as agreed between the Bank and the Treasury, are handed over to the nation. This is the sprat to catch a mackerel, as we shall see in the next chapter, when we deal with the immediate sequel. For in 1932, on the base of the £15 millions increase, the banking interests were able to increase their holding of the nation's marketable securities, or of interest-bearing "loans", by a cool £300 millions. The 1928 Act marks a second fundamental step in the evolution of privately issued currency, the first of which was taken when the early goldsmiths found it "safe" (for them) to issue bank-notes, or promises-to-pay gold on demand many times in excess of the gold they possessed. These recent rapid changes have much clarified the real issue at stake and made it possible to bring it home to the nation beyond the possibility of its being misrepresented.

What is Genuine Money To-day?

It has been necessary in this chapter to go in some detail into the kaleidoscopic changes which the empirical body of rules that does duty as our monetary system has undergone since the outbreak of the war, though much of it is familiar to the ordinary reader. But this history has involved deferring to the next chapter some of the more interesting and crucial considerations that underly these changes. Money under the existing situation has no longer the remotest resemblance to what it has ever been before. All the former ideas about good money and bad, about genuine money issued by the State and the private money put into circulation by the counterfeiter, about the duty of the State to protect the owners of money from its being maliciously tampered with and its value in goods debased, have now gone overboard. We are in an age of "monetary policy" when the value of it is continually altered, by the means well known to the banking profession, to make it worth less or more, thus to raise the pricelevel or to lower it. To stabilize its value is quite impossible without utterly destroying the pretences upon which the banking system has battened, whereas, if these were put a stop to, its value would again be just as stable as it used to be. In all this there is not given a moment's consideration to the most elementary principles of justice to the owners of money, who give up for it valuable goods and services and have a right to receive again value equivalent to that which they have given up.

CHAPTER IV

MONEY AS IT NOW IS

MONETARY Illusions

The advantage of money in use, that it enables all economic values to be expressed in terms of a common unit, is one of the greatest disadvantages in understanding its real nature. All economic transactions with which the ordinary citizen is concerned are always first translated into and accounted for in money units. Indeed, money units are often used without any qualification both for money and for such forms of property or debts as are easily convertible into money. The definition of money in this book is that it is the debt to the owner for a certain value of marketable property obtainable on demand in the country in which the money is legal tender for payment of debt. It is because ordinary citizens are never a consenting party to the initial exchange which creates money in the first instance that they have failed to see its vital national importance. All debts being contracted and expressed in money units they do not understand the significance of the debt-credit relation by which money itself comes into existence. The "credit of the nation" is not merely its power of running into debt for money to its individual citizens, but includes also its power of running into debt to its individual citizens for actual goods and services – whereby money itself originates. The fact that the debt owed to the citizens by the nation is in goods and services and not in money does not alter the sign of the transaction. It appears to do so only because the vendors receiving new money for wealth given up consider themselves paid, whereas they are not paid but owed.

All money given up by individual citizens to the nation in exchange for National Debt securities belongs as a matter of course to the nation that incurs the debt, whereas the goods and services given up by them in exchange for paper and credit money created by banks was accounted by our monetary system, up to the 1928 Act, as belonging to the issuer of the money. The extraordinary thing is that one would search in vain for any law sanctioning this accountancy as regards the major part, namely that issued as bank-credit.

A Distinction without a Difference

It will of course be objected that the banks do not and never have claimed permanent ownership of the money they issue. But in practical economics there is no longer any important distinction in this connection between a capital sum of money and the revenue it yields. The owner of a National Debt security is really the owner of the annual revenue it yields. If this is £100 a year and the interest is four per cent it is exchangeable for around £2,500, if five per cent for £2,000, and so on. To be in permanent enjoyment of the annual revenue is in practice the same as being the owner of the capital sum. So it is with the £2,000 millions or so created by bank-credit which yields to the banks an annual revenue at a bank rate of five per cent of £100 millions a year. Of this they have been in enjoyment ever since they issued the money and they still show no disposition voluntarily to surrender it to the nation. It is a quibble therefore to argue that they do not own the money they have created. If it were replaced by State money the State also could choose whether it received the capital sum, or lent it out and derived the interest from it – whether it incurred with it £2,000 millions of new expenditure, or whether it knocked this sum off the National Debt and saved the taxpayer £100 millions a year. These are only two of the many similar ways the nation would be the richer for accounting the goods and services given up by its citizens for money as the property of the nation rather than of the banks.

To terminate such a situation as now exists all that is required is for the public to look at money, not as it has so sedulously been instructed from the standpoint of the issuer who receives goods and services for it *gratis*, but from the standpoint of the user who has first to give them up for money before he can get them again. The accounting must begin one stage earlier than money to cover the transaction by which the money originated. If this is done the claim of the banks that they are using their own credit and not that of the community cannot be substantiated. It is true the early bankers thought they were, and no doubt they originally were when they lent part of their depositors' gold. At that epoch the credit of the goldsmiths stood higher than that of the government, which thought fit, when in need, to appropriate the merchants' stores of gold in the Tower without the formality of the owners' consent, and thus drove the latter to seek a safer "bank".

The Vested Interest in Creating Money

But when they began lending not gold but promises-to-pay gold or, later, under the cheque system, cheques, which are claims on the bank for money, the banks began to appropriate a credit that was not their own but belonged to the community which had to give up the equivalent goods and services to those to whom the banks extended the "credit" in the first instance. Now the argument has come round full circle. The invention of credit money enabled the banking profession to appropriate as its own that part of the credit of the community which has been termed the Virtual Wealth, and this, involving as it does the power of creating money out of nothing, could not help proving a most extraordinarily profitable business which has now become a gigantic vested interest.

Writers on money, from the conventional or issuers' standpoint, now argue, for example, that the banks are within their rights in times of economic depression, when no one wants to borrow their money at any price, and they have more "cash" than corresponds with the ten per cent safe ratio to their total deposits, if they buy property belonging to the public with the money that they issue, a transaction scarcely distinguishable from the operations of the counterfeiter. This is called "Open market operations" and, true to banking phraseology, this method of acquiring the nation's valuable marketable securities by the issue of new money is still technically called a "loan", rather than a theft.

Open Market Operations

When an ordinary citizen buys securities his stock of money is decreased, but with the banker it works exactly the other way. He increases the quantity of the money he issues by buying just as by lending. He destroys it again by selling just as by calling in a loan. To make this at all intelligible to ordinary citizens they must look at it in this way. The banking system is now a corporation which has a vested interest in the issue of some nine times as much money as it holds "cash", and if credit-worthy borrowers have not yet recovered sufficiently from being caught in the trap of deflation, and are unable or unwilling to borrow this issue from them, then the banks are within their rights in buying for themselves on the open market revenue-producing investments, paying for them by their own cheques. These the vendors pay into their respective banks creating deposits there, until the safe ratio of cash to deposits is reached.

Cash (!)

But what now is "cash"? In banking parlance "cash" is legal tender money plus credits at the Bank of England. Let us see how this worked out in 1932, just after we went off the gold-standard and the "monetary policy" was directed to raise prices and make the value of everybody's money worth less in goods, so repudiating part of the nation's debt in goods and services to the owners of the money. It began by the Treasury arranging with the Bank of England and authorizing them to issue £15 millions more of their Promise to Pay notes, under the 1928 Act. The net profit of this issue, whatever it may have been, the Treasury presumably was paid, and to this extent the taxpayer benefited. Then the Bank of England increased its "loans" (banking phraseology) by acquiring for itself £32 millions of marketable securities from the nation, and came into the enjoyment of the revenue of interest which they yield, paying for them by cheques. Whether or not the old lady who overdrew her account and sent the banker a cheque for the amount is an invention, there is not the slightest doubt about this being the normal, natural, and regular method of the Old Lady of Threadneedle Street.

The sellers of these securities in due course paid these cheques into their banks, and the latter returned them to the Bank of England thus increasing their credits at the Bank of England, which rank as "cash", by £32 millions. This great accession of 'cash' enabled them to increase their 'loans' by approximately £267 millions, much of the increase probably being due —in the still parlous condition of credit-worthy borrowers as yet insufficiently recovered from being deflated – to "open market operations". So that, between February, 1932, and February, 1933, they were able to show an increase in their 'deposits' of nearly £300 millions. After that it became rather ruinous to go to Switzerland for one's holiday, or to any other country on the gold-standard, owing to the 'exchange' being against us. At the time of writing (1934) the pound in countries still on the gold-standard is worth about 12s. But the banks between them 'acquired' some £300 millions of the nation's revenue-producing securities – or the equivalent revenue from their borrowers in so far as they may have succeeded in really lending the new money they issued – in the first year after going off the gold-standard.

Banks now Create Money to Spend Themselves

This surely disposes of the last vestige even of the excuse that the banks in 'assisting' industry by fictitious loans are a public service, for having, by deflation and suddenly withdrawing their 'assistance', put the nation's industries *hors de combat*, in order to reinflate the monetary concertina, there being now nobody else to 'assist', they have to fall back on assisting themselves. The banking system is in fact now nothing but a gigantic vested interest in the actual issue of new money by methods which still evade the law and ruin first creditors and then debtors. By the ordinary canons of commercial morality there is not a shred of difference between creating money to lend to others for interest and creating it to spend oneself, and now none is recognized either in banking morality. All of this was of course accompanied by the usual dishonest propaganda intended to distract attention from what was taking place. Newspapers called attention to the abundant credit facilities lying idle and no borrowers, and pointed the finger of scorn at those who imagined that shortage of money could have anything whatever to do with the slump!

The Banker as Taxgatherer

The 1928 Currency and Bank Notes Act, as indicated in the last chapter, has, beyond all doubt since the country has gone off the gold-standard, introduced a new principle into the British Constitution. Before, the issue of bank-notes was strictly regulated by law, but as regards the profits of the issue the nation made no claim to them. So long as they were convertible into gold, the banker made himself liable for the issue though he gave no security whatever for his solvency. Notwithstanding the fact that, stopped by the law from issuing notes, he began to lend chequebooks to such an extent that it soon became physically impossible for him to fulfil his bond, and that any attempt to make him do so on the part of a small section of the public would have plunged the nation into a financial panic, mercantile custom, if not the law, still maintained the fiction that the banker was trading with and using his own credit.

The 1928 Act, which authorized the issue of bank-notes by the Bank of England to replace the National Treasury Notes, laid it down that the profits of the issue should be paid to the Treasury. As we have seen, the issue of any form of credit money is a forced levy or tax on the goods and services of the community which it is impossible for the community to resist or escape. Parliament alone has the right to authorize and impose taxation, and this Act enables the whole constitutional position to be challenged. For as regards the relatively insignificant issue of notes. Parliament has delegated its powers to the Bank of England, which in this respect is the authorized but unofficial tax gatherer of the Government. For surely, even in law, it is not possible to maintain that a tax is only a tax when the levy is paid in money tokens, and that a levy paid directly in valuables is not a tax. For this would be as silly as arguing that a person giving up money establishes a credit, but one giving up goods and services of equal value for money does not.

Even in 1928 the foregoing was true for all the ordinary citizens, though the 1925 Act had given money a limited degree of convertibility into gold for the benefit of the foreign trader. This, however, was removed in 1931. Thus we have by Act of Parliament the King's head removed from the nation's money and in its place a bank's Promise to Pay substituted. Now this 'Promise to Pay' dates from the days when the bank-note was at once the receipt for gold voluntarily given up to the bank by its owner, and its promise to repay it on demand. By making the Bank of England's Promise-to-Pay notes legal tender in place of the National Treasury Notes, the promise is become a bogus promise. The bank-note is now only the authorized but unofficial receipt for a national tax collected on behalf of the Treasury by the Bank of England. The promise of the Bank of England can be shown to be bogus by anyone who cares to take some of these £1 notes to the Bank and demanding that they redeem their promise to pay 'pounds' in exchange for them. It is time this lying legend was replaced by the true one 'Received Value worth £1', and it is time this sinister delegation of the powers of taxation to the Bank of England by Parliament was challenged and reversed, and the note signed by the Treasury authority responsible, as the original Treasury Notes were.

The Sprat to Catch a Mackerel

But as already indicated this is not the real issue at all, which is the right of the banks by a book-keeping trick to create twenty or so times as much money as the amount for which legal tender receipts are issued. So long as physical tokens exist it is not possible to make them less than zero. But by book-keeping this obvious limitation can be got round, and in figures it is just as easy to count in negative numbers as in positive, and there is, then, no fixed number, such as zero, from which the counting starts. Money accountancy should start from the zero of no money. The real quantity of money is perfectly definite, for it is, in units of money, the worth of the real things the aggregate citizens are owed and entitled to receive on demand in exchange for the money. The fiction that only legal tender is 'really' money, and that cheque accounts are not money but claims on demand to be paid money, does not in the least affect the quantity of goods the citizens have given up for it and are owed on demand. The cheque system preserves the zero of no money for legal tender or physical tokens, but extends the accountancy to an indefinite and continually varying extent below zero into the region of minus quantities, or debts of the banks for non-existent money. Making banks keep pound for pound of national money tokens against their liabilities to their current account holders would at once stop this fraudulent accountancy.

Banks Give no Security Whatever

It is the strangest perversion of common justice that whereas the banks' borrowers have to deposit with the banks valuable securities, in the way of the title deeds to houses, farms, factories, or investments, amply sufficient to cover the eventuality of their default, the banks, trusting no one, themselves give no security whatever of any kind to their depositors. In the one case, when it becomes impossible for the creditors to fulfil their bond they are sold up and bankrupted. In the other case the banks are granted a moratorium and sufficient national money is then printed to enable them to avoid ruin. The pound for pound of national money would be the nation's security for their solvency and it could be issued to them as required, against suitable collateral security in the way of the banks' assets to cover the loan. But as a matter of fact the mere substitution of a national money for the present fraudulent private money system would produce such an almost instantaneous increase in real national prosperity that it would not be long before industry and agriculture got out of debt to the banks and were able to create and accumulate their own capital without the aid, for the most part, of either genuine or fictitious loans.

The Time-Element of Money

The philosophy of money here expounded, regarded in a strictly scientific light, may be said to put the difference between barter and monetary systems in the time-interval, that distinguishes the latter from the former, between the giving up of one kind of property and its repayment by another. Money may be considered intermediate repayment, but this does not quite cover the point, which is essentially one of time. If, in scientific fashion, we imagine the time-interval continuously reduced to zero, from a monetary system we arrive at a barter system, and the point is that this is not possible. If we make the mistake of supposing it to be so, it would be the same as supposing a community exchanging by barter in which as soon as one kind of produce were ready for use or consumption an exactly equivalent worth automatically appeared in the same place and at the same time of the kind the producer wanted in exchange. Whereas, as we know, there are such considerations as seed-time and harvest in the case of agricultural produce and their equivalents in industrial production, as well as that the producer never knows accurately what his needs will be in the interval between them. Money bridges this gap because it gives the means of obtaining continuously what is needed for use and consumption, irrespective of the spasmodic nature of production, or, by custom, of payment (wages, salaries, dividends) for engaging in production.

The Circulation of Money

Orthodox economists seem to ignore the technical and biological processes for the creation of wealth, and the principles regulating its consumption and use, in their almost exclusive concern with the entirely subordinate function of exchange or commerce, against which Ruskin in his day railed in vain. Here, as he expressed it, "for every plus there is a minus", one party to the exchange merely giving up what the other gets. They tried in the so-called "quantity theory of money" to make the exchange value of money depend inversely on its quantity 'in circulation' and directly on its 'velocity of circulation'. Their attempts to determine the first came up against the almost insuperable difficulty in a privately-issued money system of being sure exactly what the quantity in existence at any instant might be, let alone the quantity "in circulation", and they were dependent for this on such figures as the banking profession might wish the public to believe, besides unintelligently following the bankers' own methods of arriving at the information. These appear to be radically at fault, as still to be gone into, in slumping together current account and time-deposits, and slurring over the distinction between them. As regards the second, they seem to ignore the time-factors in production which it is the function of money to bridge, and they wrote as if it were the velocity of circulation of money which determined the rate of creation of wealth rather than the latter being the essential factor to which the *circulation* of money *must* conform. The mere fact of money changing hands, altering from moment to moment the identity of the individuals with money and without goods or with goods and without money – commerce in brief, including in the term all stock exchange, real estate, and other transactions involving the exchange of finished property – is not circulation at all. That term should be confined to the payments as above for engaging in production, the return to the production system of the money so paid out, in exchange for the product, and its passage through the production system until it is paid out again and the circle completed.

It is not necessary to consider this old "quantity theory" of money farther than this, because enough has been said to show that it is really a fraud. In practice neither of the two factors supposed to determine the exchange value of money were known, but only their product, and this by definition was simply the total money exchanged for goods per year, or "the volume of trade". Dividing, in this, the quantity of money by the quantity of goods gives the average price of goods, or the price index, a purely statistical figure which is not dependent on any theory at all. It may be stated at once that no quantitative theory of the value of money can possibly apply when the quantity of money in existence is being arbitrarily varied, created possibly to allow people to gamble with on margins in the Stock Exchange, possibly withdrawn from production for the purpose, and again possibly not. It is like taking seriously a set of statistical figures over a period, in which the units of reckoning were never the same from one moment to the next, or a set of measurements with someone arbitrarily altering the calibration of the measuring instruments to make them always read wrong.

The Value of Money or Price-Level

By regarding money as essentially credit in the first instance, the quantity of money is simply the quantity of goods and services with which its owners are credited, that is voluntarily going without, and that we call the Virtual Wealth of the community. Itself it is a quantity, not a rate like the volume of trade, and, without any complication at all, the exchange value of money is the Virtual Wealth divided by the quantity of money, and the price index or price-level is proportional to the reciprocal of this. It can only change (1) by virtue of there being more or less money in existence or (2) by virtue of the community, in the sense of the aggregate of its individual members, electing to go without and be credited with less or more goods. The first is the physical quantity and the second the psychical quantity. The latter depends on the number of individuals in the community and on their business and domestic habits and customs, which are conservative. It is inconceivable, if the quantity of money were reasonably constant, that the Virtual Wealth could be subject to any violent change whatever, except by some far-reaching natural or human cataclysm. In so far as the quantity of money in existence violently and suddenly changes, it produces violent repercussions on the standard of living and general prosperity, and upon the amount of goods and services people can afford to abstain from. But since the cause of this is purely external, arbitrary, and *preventable*, there seems no reason for discussing it and so over-elaborating the simple conception given here. It is rather the purpose of this book to apply it to a genuine money system using physical tokens regulated in amount to keep the price-level constant.

Some Monetary Factors

But to bring the conception into simple relation with the time-interval which it is the function of money to bridge, between the giving up of one kind of property and its repayment by another, it is necessary to know, besides the quantity of money, only the "volume of trade" or total money exchanged in the year for goods. If we call this $£V$ and the total quantity of money $£Q$, then Q/V is the time-interval required, namely the average time each unit of money is kept before it is spent. Let us suppose the volume of trade, in the sense defined, is taken as given sufficiently accurately by the amount of bills, cheques, etc., annually cleared by the Bankers' Clearing Houses. This was in 1928 £44,200 millions. The quantity of money in current accounts in these banks for that year is stated to have been, £1,026 millions. Hence so far as this part of the money is concerned the average time-interval between spending is rather more than one forty-fourth of a year, or eight days eight hours. Probably something like this period is true for money in general over the whole cycle of production and consumption. What it may be for each half separately can only be guessed. The time of one complete circulation is the product of this average interval and the number of exchanges in both halves. If it is correct that the national income was then about, £4,000 millions the average number of exchanges in the complete circulation is about a dozen.

In any case it is important to notice that this interval is a derived or secondary quantity, not in itself as informing as the fundamental conception of Virtual Wealth. The latter is measured by the quantity of money in existence divided by the price index, and this again, divided by the population, gives the average quantity of wealth (in money units reduced to the pricelevel taken as standard) which each individual of the community is voluntarily preferring to go without in order to own money. If the value of money in 1914 is taken as the standard (pricelevel = 100), it was in that year a little over £20 worth, and the quantity of goods and services this represents probably varies comparatively little however the price index may vary.

These figures, though they are only given as rough indications of the orders of the quantities in question, appear to be very much as might have been guessed from other considerations.

A Grain Currency

Man does not live by bread alone even in an economic sense, but let us suppose for simplicity that he does, and consider a self-contained community producing and consuming its own grain, harvested, say, in September, and call the harvest H in worth of money units of constant purchasing power. Then, neglecting the complication of the relatively small amount of grain that has to be always reserved for next year's sowing, and assuming consumption to be at a uniform rate, the quantity of grain always in existence as a minimum must be FH where F is the fraction of the year still to run before harvest. Thus F is o just before and 1 just after harvest, in March $\frac{1}{2}$ in June $\frac{1}{4}$, and so on. Now suppose a simple money system to distribute this harvest in which the government issues H units of money to buy it in September, and sells it again throughout the year. Then, just before harvest, the community have no money and no grain, just after reaping, H of grain and no money, and, just after selling it, H of money and no grain. This well illustrates the spasmodic character of production which it is one of the functions of money to bridge. By March the government have $\frac{1}{2}H$ both of money and of grain, and the community $\frac{1}{2}H$ of money, by June the government have $\frac{3}{4}H$ in money and $\frac{1}{4}H$ grain and the community $\frac{1}{4}H$ of money, and so on, the quantity of money in the pockets of the community always equalling in value the stock of grain in the government's granary. Note, especially, that the government has only to *issue H* units of money *once*, not every harvest!

It is of interest that something like this simple system exists as regards the distribution of grain in Latvia, the issue, called Treasury Notes, being 104 million Lats (1 Lat = 1 Swiss franc, now about fifteen to the pound) and the other money being about thirty-six millions of paper and coin and fifty-seven millions "bank credit", with a gold base of forty-six millions, in Lats. How infinitely better this is than when the government does not issue money and the producers before harvest are always in debt for some part if not the whole of the harvest which when reaped repays their debt, and leaves them again in debt during the whole or part of the period before the next. The essential physical fact is that there must always be FH of grain in existence, or the community will go short or starve before the next harvest, and that fact is not altered by bank finance, the sole social purpose of which is to keep the producers of wealth in debt so as to ensure that they work hard to repay it and do not slack. That may or may not be an economic necessity but, if so, they should be in debt to themselves, and *that* is what money really is and what it does, whoever issues it.

Economizing in the Use
of Money now Fallacious

It is the irony of the situation that the methods invented by the old banker to "economize in the use of gold for currency", by creating money without any gold, ought now to be used by the State to economize in the need for the banker (in the modern sense of minter) if the State is to continue to exist except as the perquisite of the minting profession. The idea of economizing in the use of currency dates from the days when it needed a long and precarious search for the precious metals costing on the average probably much more than they were worth. The very opposite obtains now that we understand that gold and silver money only embody in a crude and elementary form the principle of Virtual Wealth. Money is a debt owed the owner by the community. The issuer of money fades out of the picture with the goods and services he obtains for nothing by the issue and, much as he may pretend he is liable for the issue and the repayment of the debt, the debt is never and never can be repaid, but in a scientific age goes on increasing and circulating through the community, exchanging their goods and services for ever after.

We may still learn much from the foregoing illustration as to the nature of any money system. As regards the point that there is always just as much wheat in the state granaries as there is money in the pockets of consumers, many monetary reformers have averred as a self-evident proposition that there always ought to be as much money in existence as there exist goods and services awaiting sale, and we shall have to comment on this proposition later. But first notice that, on the average, one-half of the grain money, rising from zero after harvest to H just before the next, is always lying in the government's coffers, "idle and barren" as the old bankers would have bemoaned, but really for the simple reason that there is then no grain to be had in exchange for it.

Money Tokens or Book Credit?

Now, so far as concerns a state service of this character, it is clear that the government instead of keeping the money returned to them during the year might as well burn it as received, to avoid the risk of loss during keeping, and issue a new lot every autumn. Or, in terms of book-keeping instead of counters, it could issue a credit of H to the producers for their harvest, and, as the grain is bought back from them, cancel the credit. This involves a new issue of credit every harvest and its destruction throughout the year instead of a single issue of permanent money once for all. In this particular instance the credit accountancy is even truer to physical reality than the other, since the credits correspond always to the unconsumed grain and there is no money lying "idle and barren", But it is absolutely essential to notice that, if the grain were not in effect a government monopoly but was being bought by wholesalers in the ordinary way of business in an individualistic society, they could not afford to cancel the credits as they resold their grain, for the simple reason that they have not the power to re-create them next harvest. That is possible only for a government conducting the marketing. It is possible for banks because they usurp the prerogative of governments in issuing and destroying the credit of the community for goods and services given up by them. The usurpers charge interest for getting people into their debt, whereas all democratic governments would issue money to keep people out of their debt if they knew the elementary rudiments of their trade.

These remarks may also serve to illustrate the different starting points of two schools of monetary reformers; those who want genuine permanent national money issued by the state after the increase of production is ready for distribution, solely according to statistical regulation, to maintain the price-level constant, without any other let or hindrance whatever; and those who look rather to a modification and extension of the system of issuing *ad hoc* credits for definite production purposes, the credits being destroyed and re-created again at each round of the cycle of production and consumption.

The reasons why the former system is preferred in this book are many, but the primary reason is that a system that must use some form of physical counters is so much less easy to falsify than one of book-keeping. Also, as already indicated, until some such open and unobjectionable system is reverted to, and full statistical experience of it made known, there are many simple questions, such as the correct quantity of money for a given rate of production and consumption, that cannot really be answered definitely, and which, indeed, it seems to be the object of the present system to make unanswerable. Men do not live by bread alone, even in the economic sense, and in modern industrialized communities at least, but also to an increasing extent in modernized agriculture, there is a fairly constant flow throughout the year, through the whole cycle of production and consumption, of payments for raw materials, intermediate products, and services in production, balanced by equal payments for the finished products or for reinvestment. Even though production as in the illustration be spasmodic, men do not live by fits and starts. Though in the initial days of credit money, one of its functions was to facilitate the increase of production, now it is the other way and the problem is to distribute all that men are already able to produce. Under these circumstances particularly there seems no reason at all why money should not be permanent and physical, thus avoiding the risk of dishonest accountancy that can so easily occur where money is being continually destroyed and re-created.

Should Money Lending now be Permitted?

The next point of interest is that, though the Government, when it receives back the money, cannot use it to buy grain because there is then no grain to buy, there is nothing to prevent the producer, when he receives it at the harvesting, from lending part of it at interest for part of the year to someone else, who would not borrow were he not desirous of spending. Confining the consideration still to money issued in a self-contained community for the purpose of marketing a single commodity, grain, it is equally clear that the only grain the borrower can buy is that which the lender will himself require later on in the year, and if the borrower consumes it, so that it may not "lie idle in the granary", the lender cannot get it back when he wants it. All of these simple considerations may serve to raise the broad question of the physics, if not the ethics, of money-lending in general, in contradistinction to genuine investment, when the investor in effect spends his money and can only get it back by finding someone else willing to buy his investment from him. There is a growing school of sociological thought, following the best traditions of medievalism, against money-lending as such, in which the lender takes no risk, as he does when he sinks his money in a genuine enterprise with the success or failure of which his own fortune is bound up.

The more one thinks over it the more it seems as though even genuine money-lending, pure and simple, however essential it may be to preserve it in the transitional stage to the new era in order to avoid too great and sudden interference with commercial habits and ideas, would even now under a properly worked pure credit-money system be a retrograde redundance, undoing with one hand what is done with the other. Money is itself a debt of goods and services, and outside of the question of securing specific objects – such as to enable an exceptionally enterprising and capable individual more quickly to arrive at opportunities of social usefulness – lending money is merely creating a new private money debt between individuals which, if the physical circumstances were such as to justify the creation of the new debt, ought rather to be met by the issue of new money. For no one borrows money to hoard but only to be able to consume, normally, of course, for the purpose of putting into production new wealth which will only be ready for consumption or use at a later date. A money debt thus usually takes out of the market just the same amount of finished wealth as if the owner had himself spent his money and consumed what it bought, while owing to the prevailing laxity in these matters he feels quite at liberty to call in the loan and again consume what the borrower has already consumed.

Physical Absurdity of Short Term Lending

Whatever may be thought of loans of money for definite long periods, covering the reproduction of the wealth the borrower consumes, when he is in a position to restore wealth to the system before the original owner of the money recovers his money and can take it out again from the system, the practice of lending money on call or short notice is physically idiotic and should be stopped. It is merely a mathematical and not a physical possibility, due to the variable minus quantity from which the quantity of money is now reckoned, which the use of physical counters would make impossible. Because then it would not be possible, as it is now, for the owner to recover again his money without someone else giving it up. Repayments must under such circumstances balance new lending, whereas it is not too much to say that the very object of the existing system is to escape this limitation imposed by ordinary common sense.

Current Accounts and Time-Deposits

This may serve to reintroduce the point deferred from the last chapter as to the essential difference in correct accountancy between current accounts and time-deposits, which it has been the practice of the banking system to slur over and slump together. The sum of the two, or "total deposits", represents the money the bank owes their depositors on demand or short notice. When a client transfers money from a time-deposit to a current account it makes no difference to the "cash" to credit ratio, and it would appear that some of the worst falsifications of the monetary system arise from this quite unjustifiably loose procedure. Although a time-deposit is nominally only recoverable by the owner on due notice, even the stipulated period is usually not insisted upon. At the worst the bank would merely charge a "discount" for refunding the money without notice, unless itself in difficulties.

Whereas it is clear that if a depositor is receiving interest on his deposit from the bank, the bank is only paying it because itself it has lent it to some borrower, presumably at a higher rate of interest. The money is no more in the bank's possession than the gold belonging to the depositors remained in the goldsmiths' safe when they lent it out at interest. If money is defined as the debt of goods and services owed the owner of money on demand then, to arrive at the total quantity of money in existence, we must not add together the money in current accounts and in time-deposits, but reckon the former only. The money in the time-deposit has been lent out by the bank, which is paying the owner interest for doing so, and it either appears in someone else's current account or time-deposit.

If in the latter, then the same consideration applies to the new as to the original time-deposit. That is to say, in order to arrive at the total money in existence only the current accounts must be reckoned. This assumes, as is customary in this sort of rough and ready reckoning, that the money outside the banking system altogether, in the hands of the public as physical tokens, does not change, but it is in any case too small a proportion of the whole seriously to invalidate the conclusion.

How the Banker Avoids his Own Trap

It would seem probable that it is by this method that the truly frightening destruction of money that has been going on since the deflation policy of the Cunliffe Committee was started has been concealed. By slumping together the two kinds, the "Deposits" that alone are given in the banks' balance-sheets do not appear greatly diminished. Figures it is true have been published latterly that would make it appear that the ratio between current accounts and time-deposits has, since 1919, only changed from the ratio 2 to 1 then to 1 to 1 now. But they appear faked. So far as their source can be traced they appear to come from a table published in the Macmillan Committee's Report. Certainly in 1922 the statistician, H. W. Macrosty, complained that these important figures were not published by the British banking system, and he estimated the ratio as then 5 to 1, as for the eight hundred chief banks of the Federal Bank System of the United States.

However this may be, it would appear that the present i to i ratio is the lowest it is possible to bring it to. Since the banks dare not destroy the money actually lent to them by their depositors, or they would themselves be caught in the trap which those to whom they have lent money are caught in. These "time-deposits" can be demanded by their owners at short notice, and for a 1 to 1 ratio, since the money in current accounts give the aggregate in existence, they can, except by re-creating again the money destroyed, only be paid by transferring the whole of the money in existing current accounts into the current accounts of the owners of the time-deposits. The 1 to 1 ratio arrived at by deflation means that the banks have left just enough money in existence to meet this liability, and if this interpretation of the situation is correct, then it would appear that practically all the rest of the money in existence has been destroyed in their frenzied efforts "to crucify the country on a cross of gold and glut".

CHAPTER V

INTERNATIONAL ECONOMIC RELATIONS

BAD Money Embroils the Nations

The system that has grown up could not have survived so long, or have remained so long camouflaged as the opposite of what it really is, but for the complication introduced into the problems by international economic transactions. Viewed from the standpoint of a single self-contained community, the gold-standard involves an almost self-evident contradiction. It is a system in which money was supposed to have been kept of constant value with reference to gold and in which the manner of issuing new money was such that it necessarily reduces in proportion the value of the rest. For since there are no more goods and services on sale than before the issue, what is on sale is divided among more money units, so that each becomes worth proportionally less, and the new issue merely dilutes the value of the old. In practice, this fundamental contradiction resolved itself into its two parts or phases – the inflationary period when the price-level was being forced up by new issues, and the deflationary period when it was being forced down again by the destruction of money. The intermediate stage, the draining of gold out of the country as the one type of commodity arbitrarily prevented from rising in price, so reducing the "cash to credit" ratio, is the stage that brings in the international aspect of money. Bad money at home embroils the nation's affairs abroad.

International Banking

As the inevitable inconsistency underlying their system became familiar to the banking profession in different countries, there grew up a corresponding system of international banking, working hand in glove with the internal banking systems, to the mutual benefit and security of both. They thus extended the area of their operations to that of the whole civilized world, and made it much easier for them to escape detection and punishment. Whereas internal banking plays off in turn the debtor and creditor classes within the community and keeps them in perpetual strife and poverty, international banking plays off the poorer country against the richer and, by reducing the latter to the level of the former, is the real agent fomenting and perpetuating the aggressive nationalism out of which international conflicts arise. *Money, the lenders say, must find its own level. In doing so it drags down to the lowest level the standards of living both of individuals and of nations.*

In the inflationary stage, the export of goods is rendered difficult and unprofitable, owing to the high prices and the abundance of purchasing power in the home market. Whereas the import of goods, to correct the shortage of finished wealth, resulted from its having been handed over *gratis* to producers to sink in future production, is favoured because of the high prices in the home market, and the possibility of obtaining from abroad goods at the same price as before by the use of gold. In the deflationary stage the opposite obtains. The destruction of money and calling in of loans curtails employment and reduces the purchasing power of the community concurrently with the arrival on the market of the abundance of goods still in course of production, and there is a catastrophic fall of prices. Import from abroad is prevented and, instead, the goods that cannot be sold at home through the destruction of the medium of exchange are rushed to the ports for shipment abroad at any price they will fetch.

Money at Call and Short Notice

In the first stage, the banker's loans are in demand at home, but in the second, having called in his internal loans, he has lending power to lend, and his revenue in the form of interest is drying up. It is at this precise moment that the demand arises for loans to finance the export trade. In this situation, therefore, the business grew up of lending money at call and on short notice to the international bankers financing the shipment of cargoes being exported and imported, on the security of these cargoes. Clearly money created for this sort of transaction, essentially transport, can be very much more quickly recalled and destroyed than that sunk in production. By dividing the business into long term lending, and lending on call or short notice, and by increasing the ratio of the first in the inflationary period and of the second in the deflationary period, the internal bankers contrived to extract a more constant revenue by lending out the Virtual Wealth of the community, which, as regards the second source, they shared with the international bankers. Of the main items in a bank balance-sheet, on the assets side, "Money at Call and Short Notice" and "Bills Discounted" refer mainly to the international lending market, "Advances, Loans, etc." to the internal loans, and

"Investments" to what the banks have bought with the money they create for themselves under open market operations.

How the International Banker Rules the World

By alternately lending and withdrawing loans at home and withdrawing and lending them abroad, the internal and international bankers played into each others' hands, keeping the whole world in a continuous ferment, and internal price-levels always on the move. But in this sordid game the international banker soon learned that he had the whip-hand, and could absolutely control the situation and force the internal bankers to follow his lead. For by lending at any time to a country under circumstances which make it more profitable for that country to take the loan not in the form of goods but in gold, with which to buy in a third country what the loan is really required for, he could drain the gold out of each country in turn. So he could enforce deflation and a break of prices leading to prolonged economic depression there, until its workers were reduced to a more humble and less independent frame of mind. The gold-standard became not so much a device for forcing back, after inflation, the monies of all countries adopting it, and for maintaining their constant relative exchange value, as one for forcing down wages and prices in all countries to the level of the poorest and most backward.

It will be the main purpose of this chapter to try and clarify some of the excessively complicated consequences of what is euphemistically termed banking in the international sphere. From the standpoint of the professional money-lender, and from his alone, prosperity is a curse. His trade is debt, his object its creation, and his supremacy over the creators of wealth depends on the trick that his loans being fictitious they can never be repaid. National frontiers now alone bar his world dominion, so that those too must go down.

Money is National not International Debt

The first consideration about international economic transactions is that the money of any one country only has meaning in that country in which it is legal tender, or can be at demand converted into legal tender, for the payment of debts. It is a debt of that country alone, or a claim on its marts and not upon those of another nation. For the exchange ratio to remain at any definite figure without gold flowing from one country to another, in each country the value of the sales of its own money for the other country's money must be always the same as the value of its sales of the other country's money for its own money. Thus if the par of exchange between England and Germany was, as before the war, about twenty marks to the pound, £100 can only be changed for 2,000 marks if some one else wants to change 2,000 marks for £100. If only 1,800 marks for £90 were offered, then the difference £10 can only be exchanged for marks by buying 200 marks with gold. Failing that, the 1,800 marks became worth £100 or the exchange falls from 20 marks to 18 marks to the pound.

The second consideration has to do with the exchange of goods. Here for the foreign exchange ratio not to vary and gold not to flow, any excess value of imports over exports must be balanced by the country receiving the excess (1) owing for them, that is contracting a new debt as regards the rest of the world, or (2) being already owed them and in receipt of interest payment or capital repayment for debt contracted previously by the rest of the world to it. If exports balance imports (or in so far as this may be the case) they are settled by the importer in each several country paying the exporter of his own country in his own currency. An elaborate system of "bills of exchange", bill-brokers, accepting houses, discount markets, etc., explained in technical works on money, enables this to be done. The technicalities, being concerned with the means by which it is done rather than the actual purpose achieved, need not here detain us.

In order to simplify the complicated question of international economic transactions, the two propositions will now be discussed more in detail. It is only outside of these simplifying propositions that complication arises. Both reduce the problem to one as between a single country and the rest of the world taken as a whole in order to avoid having to consider the innumerable cases that would arise if we considered all the countries in pairs at a time, as of course applies to the actual transactions. The discussion is concerned to distinguish the type of transaction that has no effect on the stability of the foreign exchanges from those which disturb them.

Importers Pay Exporters of their Own Nation

The second proposition is usually taken for granted but it is well to state it precisely. It is that in any country in so far as the value of its imports is offset by the value of its exports, in its dealings with all other countries for which the same is true, the trade is really barter and does not necessarily involve any exchange of the monies of the countries at all.

In each country the importer really pays the exporter in the money of that country. The simplest case is when two countries only are concerned, for example Britain exporting herrings to the U.S.A. and the U.S.A. exporting the equivalent value of tractors to England. If the British importer of tractors pays the British exporter of herrings and the American importer of herrings pays the American exporter of tractors, each in their respective currencies, the accounts are squared.

The next most complicated case would be a triangular one with, say, equivalent values of herrings exported by Britain to Russia, of platinum by Russia to the United States, and of tractors by the latter to Britain. If we imagined each importer remitting his own money in payment of the import, Britain would have Russian, Russia would have American, and America would have British money to exchange each for its own. If one country, say Britain, took the initiative, and sent its Russian money to Russia in exchange for their American money, it could then send the latter to America in exchange for British money, and all would be satisfied. This is what in effect is done under the bill-of-exchange system. The bill-of-exchange is a sort of reversed cheque, issued by the receiver of the money and endorsed or accepted by the payer. It is in effect an I.O.U. which is exactly of the same nature as cheque money if immediately payable on demand (a "sight-draft"). But usually it is payable within three or six months from acceptance. "Discounting" such bills means creating now the money that the acceptor of the bill will have to give up later when it falls due. This is as much a creation of money, followed by its destruction when the bill is honoured by its acceptor, as the ordinary bank "loan". We are not, however, now concerned with this aspect, though it makes chaos of international trade relations.

The Balance of Trade

The foregoing proposition applies to any number of countries however interlaced the exchanges of goods and services may be, so long as in each the value of the imports equals that of the exports. Or to put it the other way, international trade and commerce can only be carried on without complications, as simple barter, when this condition obtains. But if it does, then it is clear that there can be no imports without equivalent exports and instead of the interests of exporters and importers being opposed they are the same. Literally, in each country the first are paid by the second. But if one of the group of countries imports more than it exports, for example if Russia imports more herrings from Britain than are equivalent to the platinum it exports to America, it must be cut out of the group altogether. For, in the illustrative case of each importer paying the exporter in his own currency, there would not be enough American money in Russia to exchange for the Russian money in Britain. In the simplest case the Russians would have to make up the deficit by sending gold in exchange for their money. All of this is quite simple to understand from the standpoint of money as a debt instantly repayable in goods and service on demand in the country in which it is legalized (or can at will be converted into legal tender), but entirely meaningless outside that country. The whole is an illustration of the cancellation of the mutual inter-indebtedness of nations, which modern money itself effects between individuals of one nation. The cheque system, as it operates in a single bank, is an example as between the clients of that bank, and, as extended by the Clearing House system, as between all the clients of all the banks. In every case it is only the unbalanced residuum that matters.

Effect of Loans and Repayments

The proposition can be widened to include the case of loans, extended say from country A to country B and repaid, either interest or capital, by country B to country A. We may term the latter interest repayment and sinking fund repayments, for brevity, loan service. Then the proposition is still true if, in each country, the difference between the values of exports and imports can be accounted to loans and loan service. The former will increase exports without corresponding imports, and the latter imports without corresponding exports. Thus consider a loan from country A to country B. A in effect puts B in possession of power to buy *in* A goods and services, and if B exercises this power A's exports to B are correspondingly increased without any corresponding imports into A from B. So with loan service, B repaying its loan, or interest on it, in effect puts A into possession of power to buy *in* B goods and services, whereby imports come into A from B unbalanced by any corresponding exports. In so far as this extended proposition applies to each nation severally of a group of nations, then still, however interlaced and various the relations between the several countries, the international traffic proceeds without any flow of gold and with no disturbance to the foreign exchanges. This is not to deny that these may still take place through other factors, such as tourists and others taking or sending money to be spent in other countries. Conversely, in so far as it is not true of any one of the nations, its transactions must be cut out from those of the group under consideration, and its accounts with the others can only be squared either by gold movements, exchange fluctuations, or other countervailing factors. If all the countries are on the gold-standard then there will be a flow of gold from those countries whose imports exceed exports into those whose exports exceed imports, reckoned in the manner as extended to include loans and loan service. If there is no gold-standard, the exchange will go against the former in favour of the latter.

The Foreign Exchanges

It may be useful to consider a simple case of the latter. Suppose no attempt is made to affect the exchange between two countries, either by speculators or others holding foreign currencies in preference to their own, or by tariff and bounties. Then the imports and exports, apart from those paid for by loans, loan service, or other direct imports or exports of money, *must* be of equal value, whatever their relative amounts. To take the first case again, the British importer of tractors has pounds to pay the American exporter who wants dollars, and the American importer of herrings has dollars to pay the British exporter who want pounds. The exchange ratio between pounds and dollars means and is absolutely determined by how many dollars are obtainable for £1. Before anyone in England can exchange his pounds for dollars, someone in America must possess pounds to exchange and want dollars instead. The exchange of monies is pure barter applying to the two kinds of money exactly as to any two different kinds of commodities, and the exchange rate is simply the ratio between the quantities of each offered and demanded. The only difference is that normally money has a homing instinct and each kind tends to return as quickly as possible to the place of its origin, where alone it is a legal claim for wealth and can always and instantly be exchanged for it.

It is not possible in international commerce to cross the frontier and to replace a debt for the goods and services of the one country by a debt for a similar value of goods and services of the other. The debts, that is the monies, must be exchanged, and, before anyone can change foreign money for his own kind, someone else simultaneously must want it and give up the other kind for it. It is only within the jurisdiction of one country that the banking system can create money like a conjurer producing rabbits out of a hat, and then destroy it again. People may think our bankers are singularly unprogressive in as yet not having created an international currency apart from gold, but such people are usually more concerned with their own comfort and ability to travel about from one country to another than with anything so entirely beyond their comprehension as this aspect of money. It would be but small compensation to America to have to give up on demand for international money, say, a house to a British subject, because the latter used to have a house in Britain but had exchanged it with another Briton for the money.

Gold-Standard Drags all Nations down to Level of Lowest

The ostensible object of a number of countries uniting in making their monies convertible into gold, that is adopting the gold-standard, was simply to facilitate the accountancy between nations. For if, as in the preceding example, Russia exports less platinum to the States than Britain exported herrings to Russia, the difference is made up by a shipment of gold from Russia to Britain, and the accounts were squared. But unfortunately in practice correct international accountancy under the gold-standard, operating with the entirely false accountancy within the nations severally, where money was arbitrarily created and destroyed at will, came to mean that each nation was in turn frustrated and brought back to the standard of living prevailing in the poorest and most backward. So long as a loan from one country to another is a loan of goods and services, and repayment is also in the form of goods and services no gold drain results. The citizens of the debtor country are empowered to indent on the marts of the creditor country in the one case, and the citizens of the creditor country on those of the debtor country in the other. No money passes the frontier.

Now it is of the nature of the case that the countries that lend are richer and more highly developed than those which borrow in the monetary sense. But it is almost equally of the nature of the case, when we use the words rich and poor in the original sense of wealth or wellbeing, that costs of production will tend to be higher in rich countries than in poor. At first, of course, as in the acquisitive Victorian epoch, scientific methods of production, in exposing the worker to the direct competition of the machine, cheapen these costs. It was this which enabled Britain to become the factory of the whole world. But, as such methods become general and all nations become equipped with the same labour-saving plant, the cost of production will tend to be lowest where wages are lowest, that is in the countries where the standards of living are lowest and least protected from reduction by labour unions and ameliorative legislation, such as unemployment and health insurances.

No other considerations than these are necessary to make it clear that, though the poorer countries will borrow from the richer ones in a monetary sense, the borrowers will find it increasingly to their advantage to borrow money rather than goods and services, and to expend the money in still poorer countries where costs are lowest and the things they need are cheapest. Then arises the triangular situation, of a country A lending to another B which buys not in A but in a third country C, and pays by draining gold from A to C, precipitating in A deflation and a period of prolonged economic paralysis. Thus inevitably the gold-standard acts to keep all the world as poor as the poorest nation which competes for markets.

Effect of Freeing Foreign Exchanges

Now let us examine this same case with the exchanges absolutely free to adjust themselves. If A lends money to B, B must take it as goods and services from A. Conversely if B repays a loan to A, A must take it as goods and services from B, because any attempt to buy in a third country C will put the exchange at once against the country attempting to buy and make it more profitable for the buyer to avoid exchanging money and this he can do only by buying in the country from which the money is received. Under these circumstances the exchanges come nearly to reflect, as they ought to do, the relative worth of the monies, each in its own country. The par of exchange then means the relative quantities of the various monies which, each in its own country, buys the same average amount of goods and services. To be more precise, there is on the average no economic advantage in changing money at all. In so far as individuals are under the necessity of doing so and their necessities do not cancel each other, the exchange will move against the country which, on the balance, is changing its own money to pay foreign indebtedness, so making it easier for the debt to be settled directly by the transference of goods and services rather than by exchanging money at a loss.

Usually the case is argued along the lines that it is impossible to maintain both a constant internal price-level and a constant exchange ratio abroad, and that the choice has to be made between them. But the argument here is directed to show that it is quite essential to leave the exchanges free to find their own parity, when the internal price-level has been stabilized. Let us suppose two countries in which the par of exchange reflects equal buying power of the two monies, each in its own country. So far as the argument is concerned, we may for simplicity ignore the differences of quality between the imports and exports of the one or between the exports and imports of the other country, and even suppose each country is importing exactly the same things as it exports, as indeed to some extent happens under our mad system, much to the mystification of seafaring men. Then let the one country. A, be inflated while the other, B, maintains a constant price-level, the exchanges being quite free to adjust themselves. Goods in country A are becoming dearer. This operates to check its exports and stimulate its imports. But as in both countries the importer pays the exporter of his own country in his own currency, unless the exchange rate adjusted itself, the importers in A will be paying the exporters for more goods than they have exported, while the importers in B will be paying the exporters in B for less than they have exported, which, as Euclid would say, is absurd. The device of imagining the goods imported to be the same as those exported merely makes what tends to happen clearer without essentially distorting the truth. The debts incurred by A in B, on the balance for imports in excess of exports, can only be squared by the greater quantity of A's money in B exchanging for the lesser quantity of B's money in A, since each is useless to the exporters furnishing the goods until it is exchanged for the other. But this is exactly what has really happened, for it takes a greater quantity of B's money to buy in B the same goods as before. So far from attempting to equalize the exchange any attempt to do so is to rob Peter to pay Paul, and the more quickly the exchange turns against a country debasing its money the better for all concerned. But private speculation on the foreign exchange must be completely stopped and the exchange of national money for that of other countries must also be put under direct national supervision.

Correct Use of Gold

Nor is there anything in all this in the least detrimental to gold being used as a convenient form of merchandise to correct purely temporary or spasmodic disturbance of the exchanges. For this, indeed, it is very well suited. But it must be regarded as a commodity and divorced altogether from its "gold-standard" function of producing by its outflow and inflow thirty-fold reductions and increases of the total quantity of money. A currency stabilized at a constant index number or price-level by increasing the total quantity of money, as increase of production puts on the markets increased quantities of goods for consumption, would still find a certain average holding of gold an advantage in stabilizing the exchanges. If another country with money convertible into gold began to inflate, its increased imports would be paid for by outflow of gold so long as it had any, but the gold accumulating in the country exporting to it would under this system tend to be worth less, in relation to the average of other goods, than before. This itself would be an effect of the same nature as the exchange going against the country debasing its money. But, so far as concerns the country with stable money, gold is just one of the commodities it can buy abroad with, and, apart from the convenience of using it for smoothing out spasmodic exchange fluctuations, it is free to import or export just as much or as little as may be to its economic advantage.

CHAPTER VI

PHYSICAL REQUIREMENTS OF A MONEY SYSTEM

MONEY in the New Economics

It has been necessary to go at some length into the evolution of the existing monetary system, and also to show how it is operating to keep the world in its present highly dangerous and explosive condition. During the course of this exposition certain suggestions have been made for its reform. These depend in part at least on the new and original interpretation of the physical realities of economics that was dealt with to some extent in the introduction. They are likely to be much more easily understood by those engaged in productive avocations than by those trained in outworn habits of thought, from whom, unfortunately for the world, most leaders and administrators have hitherto been selected.

It is not possible to mix these old and new philosophies any more than it is possible to mix science with witchcraft and magic, or for a modern man to think and act within the same horizon of ideas as a primitive people. Above all the new economics of abundance or the monetary system required to distribute it cannot be expounded in terms of the old economics of scarcity. In this new philosophy money itself appears for the first time in its true light, being, instead of wealth, merely a receipt for wealth voluntarily given up for it; used in short as a credit token. To-day, we allow the whole world to be held in the grip of people who have discovered how to get wealth given up to them without even printing receipts for it; in a scientifically controlled civilization the issuer of money would bear to the rest of the economic organism much the same function as the booking clerk at a railway station does to the rest of the railway service. *Just as the latter has to account for the money he receives in return for the services of the railway he distributes, the other would have to account for the goods and services he receives in return for the money he distributes.* Such a simple idea as this is the starting point of in the new era. It is true that money tickets are permanent and, once issued, go on circulating for ever without being destroyed or cancelled. But apart from this very much the same sort of considerations of ordinary common sense are involved as would apply to a railway.

There is now No Shortage of Wealth

In the new economics there is now no difficulty in creating wealth. Unemployed labour and capital are only waiting to be given orders to proceed to do so. If it were understood once and for all that, when they had done so, the money would be issued by the nation to distribute the product at the same price-level as prevailed when the costs in connection with their production were incurred, nothing else would be necessary to ensure that all the unemployed labour and capital would permanently be put into full productive operation. From that moment the nation, as a matter of course, would be working all out for the creation of wealth for consumption and use as, during the war, it was working all out for the creation of wealth for destruction. It is, in the author's opinion, an exaggeration to suppose that the time has yet arrived when it is impossible usefully to employ any part of the labour and capital available. No doubt a considerable re-orientation of the productive system to meet changed conditions may be required, but for a long time to come we shall have full use for everybody and everything able to assist in the reconstruction of the world.

But those who wish to know further as to the principles to be observed in order to achieve this result must be prepared at this stage to cut the painter altogether and part company from the old metaphysical school of economists, who realized the underlying physical implications of the subject no more than the technically untrained man. To a scientific man, it is well-nigh incredible that a body of men, posing in this very subject as experts, should for nearly a century have failed to distinguish clearly between the consequences of genuine lending and of pretending to lend by creating new money as "bank-credit".

Motive

The difference between the economist and sociologist on the one hand, and the scientifically trained mind on the other, could not be better illustrated than in the treatment of human motive, with which it might have been expected that the former would have contributed more than the latter. The economist saw in it nothing deeper than desire for "profit" on the part of a competitive horde of acquisitive individuals. The sociologist fills volumes with the discussion of " – isms", personifying in the time-honoured guise of gods and demons, and giving capital letters to imaginary protagonists conjured into existence to explain nothing more human than errors of counting and economic swindling, grosser (because more universal), than the falsification of weights and measures. The scientist takes it for granted that, in an individualistic society, unless men can obtain a livelihood somehow they must cease to exist by the ordinary process of starvation, and had better not have been born. He recognizes, however, that there is no power on earth, or for that matter in hell, which can permanently obstruct men from availing themselves of all that their knowledge and skill can derive from nature for their sustenance, thus arriving at a broad and satisfactory theory of war, revolution, sabotage, and social strife, which fits this age as a glove.

The Existing Wealth

It may be useful to start this brief survey of the obvious physical principles that must be observed if money is to play its correct role in an individualistic community, with a trite but physically important proposition. If we contemplate everything of economic value that distinguishes the present civilization from any former one we may be sure that it must have been produced and is not yet consumed. In our advanced civilization it is seldom that people either find or actually make the things that they want. In practice men usually confine themselves to some specialized form of labour, relying for the rest on the activities of others. This is known as the division of labour and, though in the sociological sense this has more and more come to mean a social scale with an over-worked middle and voluntary or involuntary leisure at either end, it is the purely economic sense of the phrase that is intended.

The things produced directly by their owners for use and consumption, as being exceptional, may be accounted as produced by people employing themselves, who however require sustenance while doing so no less than those employed to produce for others. It is natural therefore to distinguish two main *purposes* of wealth, according to whether it is consumed in just living, in "Consumption Absolute", as Ruskin put it, or in producing new wealth for future use and consumption.

Consumption for Production and for Leisure

The distinction is loosely expressed in the ordinary monetary connotation of the terms spending and earning. But, from a physical point of view, both these actions equally entail consumption of consumable wealth and the use of non-consumable or permanent wealth, however much the things consumed or used, either in just living or in producing for the future, may differ in detail. But it is not only this which accounts for a certain confusion of thought in this subject. In an Age of Want most people asked no more than, and were glad if they got as much as, would maintain them in a reasonable state and comfort for the purpose of production. Wages, or, for that matter, salaries, at least in the lower grades exposed to competition, have never been anything else but fixed by the average remuneration required to enable the worker to carry on his avocation efficiently, in the manner customary, and with the standard of living and the social status usual to that type of avocation, and to suffice to rear a family or provide training for a new generation to carry on the same occupations. Admittedly there has always been a considerable elasticity in determining the remuneration, as well as in the degree of comfort and satisfaction different people derive from the same remuneration, according to an immense range of individual circumstances and aptitudes.

But in an Age of Potential Abundance, with the increasing opportunity for leisure afforded by the increasing efficiency of the production process the distinction is becoming of much greater importance, and it seems desirable to separate this use in "just living", the real leisure use, from the other more sharply. Leisure is becoming no longer a luxury or old-age reward, but a universal economic necessity, outside of the production process, and quite apart from what the term has usually been taken to mean – sufficient recreation to maintain the worker in mental and bodily fitness. Death alone may be expected to rid the world of those who, often doing little enough themselves, yet regard a wage above the subsistence level as an unhealthy symptom and in need of financial correction by deflation. There can be no doubt whatever that, psychologically, this was at the bottom of the disastrous financial policies the country has pursued since the war.

Consumable and Capital Wealth

But on the physical side there is a very real division of wealth into two categories also, quite outside the one just stressed, which though also purposive or functional in character, does depend on entirely different physical characteristics. It is the distinction between wealth that is consumable and that which is not. It is this that the new economics has stressed. The fundamental importance of it was completely outside the comprehension of the old. The existing confusions especially in regard to the nature of what is meant by the chameleon-like term Capital, including all its derivations and ramifications in the sociological controversies concerning "Capitalism", seem to have their origin mainly in the neglect of this essential difference. Thus to Marx (1859) "The wealth of those societies in which a capitalist mode of production prevails, presents itself as an immense accumulation of commodities". Whereas to a new economist guided by the energy theory of wealth, as already hinted, an immense accumulation of commodities would simply rot. It is quite impossible and moreover very unprofitable to try to accumulate enough wealth even to last the individual through old-age. He is in daily need of fresh wealth, and the accumulation is of debt not wealth. Moreover these capital debts have the identical peculiarity of money itself as a debt. They can never be repaid!

To the individual, it is hardly of importance whether the claim he possesses on the communal revenue of wealth is a pure debt, like the national debt, providing him with an income provided by taxation of the incomes of himself and others, or whether it derives from the output of a revenue-producing enterprise to which he has lent or entrusted money and so helped to start. But even if it is the latter, the productive capital of the enterprise itself is usually almost entirely worthless, except as a scrap valuation, if not used for the particular purpose for which it was provided, or if better means of supplying the need are invented.

Capital Debts not Repayable

Productive capital in this sense is only wealth to the individual because (1) it may be exchanged for wealth with another individual or (2) because he can charge hire or rent for the use of the plant he has helped to provide. Unless nationally owned, from the community's standpoint it is, like the national debt, merely a source of revenue to the owner of the debt at the expense of the rest of the community. Both equally are physically irrepayable.

The essential consideration underlying the foregoing is that though the two categories of wealth may exchange among individuals, the one cannot be changed into the other at will. The change can only go one way, from consumable wealth into permanent wealth, by feeding and maintaining the producers of wealth. It is a matter of choice whether the producers shall raise pigs and grow corn or build factories, and the maintenance required by the one type of producer is not essentially different from that required by the other. But the choice once made is irrevocable. From the standpoint of the nation, the exchange of one sort of wealth for the other, whether it is A or B who own the one or the other, is not of importance. The one owns the wealth and the other the debt exactly as in the exchange between wealth and money.

Energy Considerations

This physical distinction between consumable and unconsumable wealth is at bottom an energy distinction. In the class of consumables proper, such as food, fuel, explosives, and similar commodities, we deal with things which are useful because they are consumable or destroyable. In the category of permanent wealth we deal with things that are useful because they are durable and resist destruction. In this class it is usual to distinguish the permanent wealth that people make use of and require in their personal and domestic lives from that which appertains to their avocations in the capacity of producers, and to which the term 'productive capital' may be without ambiguity applied. For the former 'personal possessions' suffices. Before leaving the point let us go a little farther into why this distinction is so fundamental. The physical qualities contrasted are, superficially, ability to change and ability to endure, or changeability and durability, but this only conceals a deeper meaning. The first class by their change provide the flow of energy which actuates animate beings and inanimate mechanisms alike, but, for the second, just because they are required to endure, it is the other way. They are not used as internal reservoirs or sources of energy at all, but must be capable of withstanding change or alteration when subject to external force or stress. For spontaneous change in the material sphere only occurs accompanied by a change of energy analogous to that of water running downhill. Our distinction at bottom is between the things that can change, yielding such a flow of the energy that actuates life, and those that can resist change when subjected to energy attempting so to flow (force or stress).

In practice we distinguish, in border line cases, by – the function; that is to say by which of the two contrasted qualities is the useful one. Clothes, and the like, which are required to last as long as possible, are considered permanent, though for these fashion operates to shift them more over into the consumable class than necessary, the motives of the producer and the consumer being (in our mad world) antagonistic. Whereas however tough a beef-steak may be it is only useful in so far as it is consumable, and in so far as it resists digestion it is undesirable.

Productive Capital not Distributable

In this sense of Capital, as the unconsumable product of the consumption of consumable wealth, there is no distinction, for example, between a house used as a private dwelling and one used as a factory. Both are the products of the expenditure of work or energy, and in so far as they may be sources of energy themselves (by falling down or catching fire) are undesirable. But from the standpoint of there is this important distinction, that a private house comes into the consumers' mart as one of the commodities required for the use of consumers, whereas the factory does not. Its purpose is intermediate, as Ruskin remarked of Capital, and it never leaves the production system at all. It may change hands within the production system, but that is of no particular national significance so far as the accountancy reflecting its existence is concerned. Yet both are essentially identical so long as we consider only their mode of production. This no doubt was in the mind of J. S. Mill in his statement "The distinction between Capital and Not-Capital does not lie in the kind of commodities, but in the mind of the capitalist, in his will to employ them for one purpose rather than the other". Nevertheless when he has made up his mind and acted upon his decision a very important distinction does enter. It has been common since the day of Adam Smith to refer to a stock of commodities and plant, mentally earmarked for use in production, as Capital, and from this to extend the use of the word to money intended for this purpose.

It is impossible in economics to make watertight logical definitions or distinctions universally applicable in all cases. Even in mechanics the laws become different when we deal with velocities comparable with that of light, though within the range of practical engineering these complications are, as yet at least, completely without significance. But there must be a definite consistent use of the terms within the range, often quite narrow, to which the argument applies. It is far more important that they should have a narrow known and definite meaning than that their meaning should be made so wide and vague as to cover every conceivable contingency. For then, as in political and sociological controversies, they may mean half-a-dozen different things at different times in the course of a single argument. So with Capital, it would probably now be much better never to use the word at all.

Capital under Communism and Individualism

From the standpoint of the present book the use of the term is confined to the unconsumable product of consumable wealth used for the production of wealth, and it is considered as the sub-category of permanent wealth, distinguished from private possessions by its function in production. We are not concerned with intentions but the physical consequences of actions. It is only in this sense that the controversies concerning nationalization of the means of production, distribution, and exchange, and the differences between Communism and individualism have any real meaning. Forms of government have far less significance than people are apt to suppose. Thus the necessity of capital in the above sense, in general just in proportion as civilization advances, no one now questions. Every new advance in production is due to something analogous to the evolution of the plough into the tractor, demanding more and more people being set aside and maintained while producing and keeping in order the plant required for production, but not actually producing anything whatever that the ultimate consumer requires.

In a Communist state this is no less true than in others. There, the Government, as the owners of everything, take as much as they require not only for their own services but also for the provision of new capital, and the actual producers then get anything of the consumable and privately usable wealth that may be left over. In an individualistic society, for which we are exploring the role that money has to serve, the capital is provided by "investment", which means that people instead of consuming all they earn in their private or personal capacity empower others to expend it in revenue-producing enterprise, upon the output of which they acquire a lien or claim. But, after that, they can only get their principal back in any form at all useful to them by exchanging for new wealth their claim with someone else.

The consequence of this is that, in any modern individualistic State, there is always a very great deal of production going on which adds nothing directly to the products people purchase in their capacity of consumers, and which has to be accounted for by "investment" or some form of "saving", in which titles to consume are surrendered by their owners and transferred to others. Moreover this part of the expenditure is nationally, quite irretrievable and irrepayable.

All Costs of Production are Distributed to Consumers

It does not in the least affect the accountancy that this "capital" consumption is intended to lighten the labour and cheapen the costs of future production, and, if successful, does actually do so. In physics there is neither interest nor discount, neither lending nor borrowing. All these only refers to mutual arrangements as to ownership which people may choose to make among themselves. Neither do the various elements that make up cost or price enter into the physical accountancy, nor such distinctions as between the relative proportion of raw material, labour, overhead charges, profit, interest, and rent, or between wholesale price, retail price, cost price, sale price, and the like. We are not concerned with how the cost or price is divided among the various individuals participating, but merely with the total, being very sure that whoever receives it, and in whatever capacity, will enter into full individual enjoyment of it, whether it is earned or unearned, just or unjust, for positive or for merely negative and permissive services. Though many such things, of course, may make a great difference to the social wellbeing of a community, and, in particular, to the relative proportion that an individualistic society may elect to use its wealth on personal consumption and use or in productive expenditure, these things are all *subsequent* to the question of as an accounting mechanism.

Production for Consumers

Let us separate the two essential functions which are always going on together, so as to see each by itself, and suppose we are dealing with a system neither increasing nor decreasing its output, and with money at a constant price index of purchasing power. As regards the production and consumption of wealth for private and personal use we may divide the circulation proper of money into two halves, the production and consumption halves of the cycle. The two halves of the circle join (1) where money is paid out from the production half as wages and services, for putting wealth into the production side, and so it finds its way into the consumers' pockets (2) where the money is paid back by the consumers into the production system to buy the product they have produced in an earlier equivalent period of production. The circulation of the money is endless, with only the consumable, and privately-usable wealth, produced flowing out at (2) for consumption. The total aggregate paid out in respect of the production of any definite quantity of things produced is the price, and it is only because this money is paid out that the product can be bought and the same money used again to produce a fresh quantity. The same money goes round over and over again distributing an endless succession of goods and services to the consumer.

As already indicated, it is a beginners' mistake to imagine that all the costs incurred by industry are not distributed to buy the product. It is utterly incorrect to suppose that there is any difference between them. Overhead charges, interest, rent, and profits no less than wages, salaries, and costs of materials, all are payments to individuals who do not hoard them in their stockings, but spend or invest them, in their private capacity as consumers, just exactly the same as other people. As regards this one purpose, production for and distribution to the ultimate consumers, the costs incurred balance the costs distributed.

Production for Producers

But when we consider the second purpose, production of capital, the product is never distributed to consumers at all, but remains its whole useful life in the production system. When a factory is built it is paid for by people, instead of going to the consumers' mart to buy things for their personal use and consumption, returning it direct to the production system, and authorizing the producers to expend it again as wages, etc., to build the factory, but the factory never is distributed to consumers and never can be. This may be expressed by saying that investment or saving by-passes the consumers' mart. The money circulating, instead of taking out the same amount of wealth as it puts in at every revolution, now circulates through the production system twice creating fresh goods, but only takes them out once, resulting in an increase of wealth in the production system. But this increase is "productive capital", useless for the consumers' requirements and, as a matter of fact, it is never distributed at all.

The Accumulation of Debts

The productive capital is built up by the creation of a permanent and irrepayable debt owned by the investor and owed to him in perpetuity. The same we shall soon come to see applies to every increase in the quantity of consumers' goods in course of production, as well as to the fixed capital, and this is the most important error of accountancy hitherto made by money economists, for until this is understood it is quite impossible to maintain a fixed value for the money or a constant price-level. Both on account of increases of fixed capital and replacements and renewals of obsolete or outworn plant, as well as on account of the increase in goods *in course* of production in an expanding era, if the expansion is not to be ephemeral, the production system distributes *far more* money than the money it receives for the products it distributes, and the difference is the accumulating capital debt, under which all nations alike are now groaning.

Solution of the Unemployment Problem

The immediate problem that has to be solved is to bring back at once into useful production the whole of the available unemployed labour and capital. The most conservative estimate is that in this country a twenty-five per cent increase would at once result. This means that in a few months everyone would on the average be twenty-five per cent better off than before. But the real increase that would result, if production were no longer throttled by money manipulation, cannot possibly be estimated from the present figures, as so much of the output is now distributed by piling up redundant and superfluous distribution costs, and this would no longer be necessary. It is perfectly correct to issue new money after the increase in the rate of production has been proceeding long enough for the increased quantity of goods to appear on the market. The retailers then have new goods equal in value to the new money issued to distribute them. But it is quite wrong to issue it as a debt to industry in order to enable the new production to be *begun*. That is precisely analogous to setting up a booking office before the railway is built and financing the building of the railway by the forward sale of tickets.

Cost of Increasing Production not Repayable

A simple illustrative example may serve to make this vital point clearer. Suppose a weekly additional distribution of a million pounds' worth of goods is desired, and that it takes thirty weeks from start to finish of production before the first new million pounds' worth appears for sale, after which there will be a similar amount appearing every week. If the costs of production are uniform over the period of production, then the appearance of the first new million pounds' worth of wealth corresponds with the expenditure not of a million pounds but of fifteen million pounds – in general, of half the product of the time in weeks and the quantity produced per week. Besides the finished product, there will be thirty weeks' production of unfinished products ranging from zero value at the beginning to full value at the end, and, on the average, of half the value of the finished product. All of this is taken from the value of the existing money by extending credit to the producer without anyone giving up anything at all. The money loses in value in proportion to the increase because the new issue takes out of the market the equivalent of finished goods without putting any back into the market. While, as regards the fifteen million pounds' worth of intermediates it puts in, *that quantity must remain there for ever after*, as much being put in as comes out, unless the new increased scale of production is to be reduced again to what it was at first.

The case is entirely analogous to starting to distribute oil by means of a new pipeline, and omitting to account for the quantity necessary to fill the pipes. Always that amount more of oil must be put in than comes out, so that this part of the fluid saleable wealth has to be accounted in the monetary system exactly as fixed capital and paid for by permanent investment, in which the consumers' mart is by-passed and the money paid out of the production system is put back directly into it without taking out anything from it.

Exchange of Owners Contrasted with Creation of Wealth

Before leaving the complexities appertaining to the exchanges between wealth and money, slurred over rather than elucidated by the vague term "circulation", which have led economists into all sorts of impressions anent its "velocity" and the changes consequent upon the increases and decreases thereof in increasing and decreasing the rate of production of wealth, we may, for completeness, consider a few of the less essential operations. The division of the cycle into two parts, a producers' side and a consumers', side, is a device to eliminate the unessential exchanges, and it remains to consider these. They are of the nature of changes of identity of individual owners of property. On the consumers' side, all sorts of exchanges are going on mainly in regard to permanent possessions, sales of houses, estates, furniture, and the same is true, on the production side, with regard to plant, factories, and investments representing ownership in, or debt-claims upon, the production system. Nor does it seem to be important that individuals owning private property may exchange it for capital investments and vice versa, for in such cases the owners exchange sides leaving the wealth where it was. The circulation of money proper is distinct from all such mere exchange of ownership in this, that it is essentially an exchange of services for the creation of new finished wealth, and it is only in this exchange that new wealth arises.

The Quantity of Money cannot be Calculated

But the complexities show that it is not possible to calculate beforehand exactly how much money must be issued to distribute any given increase in the rate of production. One cannot simply say there must be always as much money as there are goods for sale. A similar point, called attention to by recent writers, is the greater quantity of money "absorbed" in the production system through the growing complexity of methods of production and the number of different organizations handling in series the wealth in course of manufacture, which is one of the consequences of the division of labour. We have to avoid endless calculations of this character.

The habits and customs prevailing both among producers and consumers cannot be eliminated from the question as to the quantity of money that ought to exist to distribute, at a constant price-level, any given output, or how that must be increased as the output increases. Thus, in the given illustration, it would only require a million pounds of new money if, after the system had settled down at the increased output, it took a week on the average for the money after its presentation at the consumers' mart to arrive there again. It is hardly possible even to guess this, from such data as may exist concerning a monetary system in which the quantity is reckoned from an always varying minus number, and in which the amount in existence is unknown because of the slurring over of the distinction between current and time-deposits. For similar reasons, the amount of genuine investment necessary, as a preliminary building up of the system to a higher output, is completely incalculable. It depends entirely on innumerable average factors, none of them very definitely known, relative to the nature of the increased production which the public demand, again unknown in advance.

The Price Index Determines the Quantity of Money

Fortunately it is entirely unnecessary to go further into these unknown factors, because the price index itself, under the system described, regulates the rate at which the new money would be issued. Postulating money only created, or if necessary destroyed, at the bidding of statisticians watching the price movements, and then issued to consumers as a relief from taxation, the price index would be controlled on the same principles as the speed of an engine is controlled by the engine driver. The latter could not possibly tell beforehand the integrated effect of the factors affecting the speed of the train, such as the gradient, the efficiency of the engine, the temperature and pressure of the steam, and so on. He simply opens the throttle if he wants to go faster and shuts it down if he wants to go slower, leaving the rest to his fireman. The production of new wealth under the most efficient and rapid processes can safely be left to the technologist.

All that is necessary is to have a system of creating new money if the price-level tends to fall and unsaleable goods to stack up, and to destroy it if they get scarcer and prices tend to rise. This is quite impossible under the existing banking system, but quite possible under a rational, scientific, and national system, designed in accordance with the physical realities to which the production and consumption of wealth must conform. To imagine otherwise is to attempt to preserve a system in which money is issued not to distribute wealth but as a source of revenue. If there is one lesson that the history of money enforces, it is that when its issue is used as a means of enriching the issuer, whether the issuer be the State, the bank, or the counterfeiter, it is the most disintegrating and dangerous power ever invented by man. If there is any such thing as corporate will or corporate sense of danger in a community, it is imperative this lesson should be learned before it is too late.

The Wasteful Costs of Distribution

But before leaving this subject it may be stressed again how large a part of the present effort of humanity is directed to the piling up of all sorts of unnecessary distribution costs to distribute the product, and enable everyone to share in the limited output, that is entailed by our fundamentally false monetary system. If these were eliminated, as they naturally would gradually be eliminated, by having always sufficient money to distribute all that can be made, we may look not for a twenty-five per cent increase of prosperity but for a four- or five-fold increase. As Sydney Reeve stresses in his writings, over eighty per cent of the cost is piled up under "commercialism" by entirely unnecessary competition for the *sale* of goods, whereas the costs of their manufacture are fined down to a fraction of one per cent. This undoubtedly is the gravest consequence of the orthodox economists mistaking the exchange of goods for their creation and not bothering very much about the latter at all.

The Rôle of Money Summarized

Summarizing this account of as the accounting mechanism, we find, taking the wide definition of costs explained (p. 149), that everything that exists of wealth of use to consumers is accounted or paid for by the true circulation of money, through the production and consumption systems, the money being paid out from the former for services in producing wealth and back again into it to take the wealth produced out. The existing wealth is the difference between what has been produced and what has been consumed, and this is continually changing owners by means of the hither and thither movements of money among individual consumers, apart from and without effect on the true circulation. With regard to what exists of wealth of use to producers, which is subject to the same perpetual exchange of owners by similar movements of money among producers without effect on the true circulation, and which also comes into existence in the same way as the consumers' wealth by this circulation, it is not, strictly speaking, accounted or paid for, but the costs of production accumulate as a permanent debt-charge on the production system. Exactly the same is the case for all the consumers' wealth in course or process of production, and the fact that this will ultimately be distributed to consumers makes no difference whatever to the accounting, as economic systems have to function continuously and for ever without being wound up. On the other hand, money itself is an asset in drawing up the balance of costs, on account of the fact that its possessors accept and regard it as payment in full, though in fact it is a promise to pay in the future. To this extent what is given up for it in the way of goods and serviees – the Virtual Wealth – is available to pay part of the costs incurred in the production system, but it can only be in general a small part even of the particular costs last considered, namely those sunk in the wealth in course of production. No scheme of monetary reform can be correct, or any money system sound, in which all the existing wealth cannot be accounted for in some such manner as the foregoing.

CHAPTER VII

DEBTS AND DEBT-REDEMPTION

Age of Power rather than of Machines

The older conventional ideas as to human progress, that it results from the benefits of human association and the division of labour, making each member of the community able to contribute, when engaged in a specialized form of occupation, much more to the common fund of wealth than would be possible if everyone had to provide independently for his own requirements, while true enough as far as they go, hardly touch the origins of the fundamental step forward in progress attained in what should be called the scientific age. Tools in the broadest sense have always been considered the real civilizers, increasing the efficiency of their human users in the various tasks of life. But that stage we have altogether outgrown. People who talk about the Machine Age are putting the cart before the horse. Modern machines are usually stronger, more tireless, and more accurate imitations of specialized productive functions of men; and have to be fed just like men. Unless energized they are dead as any corpse. Though men have not yet learned to feed directly on fuel, during the war some tropical river steamers are said to have been run on monkey-nuts, and, after it, the American farmers of the Middle West are reputed to have been advised to use their wheat as fuel to keep up the price. Scientifically, there is less distinction between manufacture and machino-facture than is commonly supposed. In both it is the energy that is the prior consideration. Whether it is derived from a man or beast, fed on food, or from a machine fed by fuel, is of minor import as regards the object, which is the production of wealth.

Men in the economic sense, exist solely by virtue of being able to draw on the energy of nature. Primitive civilizations were almost entirely dependent on its flow. They utilized the sunshine to raise food and rear draught-cattle and drew on the winds to propel their vessels, and to some small extent also on rivers to drive their waterwheels. But these are now supplemented by a store of energy laid down in fuel from days before man's footprint had appeared on the world. Thermodynamics has taught us how to convert the heat it furnishes on combustion into mechanical power. The primitive labourer was the intelligent transformer of the flow of energy in sunshine. The modern engineer has widened the function, to a considerable extent displacing the labourer from production. But no man creates the energy, however much it may appear that he creates wealth. Wealth, in the economic sense of the physical requisites that enable and empower life, is still quite as much as of yore the product of the expenditure of energy or work. But now it is largely produced by fuel-driven machinery, embodying the essential movements required for each step of the production in an automatically recurring cycle, rather than by individuals working under their own volition and power. Nature has been enslaved and men may, indeed must, be free.

Money Unrepayable National Debt

In this book we are primarily concerned with as the accounting and distributing mechanism, enabling generalized and social production to go on smoothly, combining the advantages of human association and the division of labour with the distribution of the product for individual and personal use and consumption. There is not the slightest doubt that the invention of money, displacing early patriarchal and feudal forms of communism, originally added enormously to the liberty of the individual. The modern tendency towards communism is entirely due to the fact that the primary function of money, the distribution of socially produced wealth, has been replaced by an entirely subordinate and alien one – how to issue money so as to make it a source of revenue to the issuer, and to bear perennial interest. This might be more readily intelligible if those who gave up wealth for money received the interest paid on the issue, but instead they pay it! It comes into existence by the simultaneous appearance of two equal items on the two sides of a bank-ledger, whereby on one side the borrower is credited with the sum borrowed and on the other debited. Taxpayers have so far failed to notice a similar but opposite peculiarity of accountancy in the national accounts. They receive each year demand notes purporting to show the amounts spent on services, the largest items on which are Local Government and Education, each costing £48 millions. But the largest item Bank Services £100 million, or thereby, is omitted. Similarly, in the Revenue accounts, the corresponding item "Interest on goods and services levied as bank-credit" fails to appear!

Capital Debts Unrepayable.
"Saving" Conventional

Apart from this irregularity, we have seen that while the circulation of money through the production and consumption halves of the cycle accounts correctly for the production and distribution of consumables, using the term to connote the wealth of use to consumers, it accounts the production of capital in the production system itself as a debt to individual investors, and these debts accumulate continuously and can never after be repaid, because they represent expenditure on things that are never distributed and, if they were, would be quite useless to the investor.

It is interesting that precisely the same mistake, making money a debt to private firms when it is irrepayable by its very nature, is, with respect to capital, also at the root of all the stale political and sociological controversies between capitalism and socialism. As a heritage of the unscientific and muddled economics of the Victorian era, the most extraordinary confusion persists in political circles on this question in connection with nationalization and similar schemes, and to these we shall have to revert. But, unless individuals prefer to trust a benevolent State to support them in old-age, they must "save" and all this saving business is conventional – lending a surplus of income over expenditure in order to get it back later and, in the meantime, a revenue from it as interest. But there is no wealth available, outside of the flow or revenue of wealth from the production system. This is real. All the rest is mere accountancy between debtors and creditors. Claims are accumulated on the revenue of wealth both as regards the use of productive capital, derived from the hiring of it out by the owners to the users, and on the revenue of the State, raised by taxation, to meet the service of loans raised by it. These loans are almost entirely for non-revenue producing expenditure, namely destructive wars for the greater part and necessary national improvements and developments for the smaller.

Necessity of Constant Price Index

Now this, without any other argument whatever, is sufficient to dictate that no monetary system can be honest or worthy of the confidence, either of the community or of other nations having economic dealings with it, that does not maintain an invariable price index. This is becoming every day more obvious through the bitter experience of the war and post-War epoch. Before people understood the insidious methods of swindling through keeping the price-level always on the move, there were plenty ready to argue that, if the costs of production fell through scientific improvements in manufacture, the price of goods ought to fall to the same extent. In that way every debt is subtly increased in its burden and the creditor put into the possession of an uncovenanted benefit, quite outside of and additional to what is in the bond as regards interest payment and capital repayment. Once one allows this, then the economic system simply becomes a cockpit for the struggle of wits, in which the agents and representatives of the creditor class are out, like the banks, to get something for nothing. This can only come by those who produce wealth setting aside more than before to serve the same nominal amount of debt, and, therefore, can only be derived by a corresponding reduction in the share of those producing it.

It will therefore be taken for granted that the money of the future must be of constant purchasing power in terms of the average, sufficiently nearly, of the things it is used to buy, from one century to another, before any real advance is possible from the present disgraceful bear-garden of perpetual conflicts nominally between 'capital' and "labour", but in reality between creditors and debtors, which the national creative organization has been allowed to become under the existing dishonest economic and monetary system.

How the Workers would Benefit

It will of course be asked at once, at least by those who want change, how, under such a system, the worker will benefit by the cheapening of the cost of production due to future improvement. It is easy to see that he, to this extent, loses the benefit if he has to share with the mass of pre-existing creditors the benefit that would arise from lower prices.

On the other hand, if costs are prevented from falling as the conditions in industry improve, producers are guaranteed a market for their maximum output, so long as it is what the public arc actually demanding. There is no limit to the issue of new money, if properly carried out, so long as unemployed labour and capital are available. This unlimited demand for labour and capital would restore the bargaining power to labour without any need for, and far more effectually than, collective action, the only effective weapon of which, the strike, actually strikes most directly at the standard of living of the workers, by sabotaging the output out of which they as well as the creditors are paid. Usually the workers having less reserves than those who have accumulated savings, suffer most by this sort of warfare. Whereas with the lowered costs of production resulting in a greatly increased turn-over, and the rising competition among employers for the whole of the available workers (as during the war), wages must rise until the latter obtain a fair share of the economies effected by increased output. At the same time, the principle underlying the new money system should be enforced with regard to new capital debts. It should not be possible, by a stroke of the pen, for any company to increase its nominal indebtedness to its shareholders and issue to them new shares without their contributing the full value in fresh capital. But it is only right that those who take the risk of loss in providing capital for industry should participate with the workers in increased prosperity. These points are however really covered by making all debts terminable after a definite period, a scheme which lies outside the r61e of money proper, but which will be reverted to at the end of this chapter as an essential feature of the new outlook on these questions which the physical understanding of them gives.

Regulation of Money by Price Index

Thus we have reached the point that the first consideration of national or general well-being is a money that always purchases the same average amount of the things it is employed to purchase. Honest people have everything to gain and nothing to lose by honesty. Although it would not be true to pretend that as yet the ideal way of fixing the price-level has been elaborated, it is a problem that could safely be left to a disinterested bureau of statisticians, analogous in function to the bureaux of standards, or, in this country, the National Physical Laboratory, which undertake the absolute determination of the standards of weight, length, and volume, and check the actual weights and measures by which economic transactions are effected. There is, in fact, already sufficient experience of the determination of price-levels and index numbers, by the Board of Trade and various other institutions, to make it quite certain that no serious difficulty would arise in practice.

It must be remembered that, by absolutely prohibiting the continual arbitrary variation of the quantity of money at each instant in existence, upon which "banking" now depends, and making its quantity known and definite, the real cause of the disastrous fluctuation of the price-level would be removed at the start, and it is quite absurd to argue from what has been happening in the past as to what will occur in the future. Obviously it is impossible to maintain a constant price-level under a banking system, in which money is arbitrarily created and destroyed by extending and withdrawing it in the form of loans or credits to industry, which loans can only be sunk in preparations for future production, and out of which both interest and profits must be earned. But, if money were only issued to consumers, as a remission of taxation, by the nation so soon as finished wealth awaited sale over and above that which can be sold by the existing money without fall of price-level, then appreciable changes in the latter could not and would not occur.

A Simple Price Index

There remains, it is true, the technical question as to which pricelevel to fix, and how it is to be computed, but in the stabilized economic world, which would result, the question seems of secondary importance in comparison with the advantage of fixing the price of any reasonable representative average of the things which the money is used to buy. Cut out the creation of money as a means of earning interest and create it for consumers, and the economic system will enter into definite equilibrium relations between all the various factors which determine relative prices of the different categories of the immense variety of things bought and sold. It would become a highly conservative and stable system, completely unrecognizable from what it is now, with the money continually being drained out from one part to be injected into another, and, all the time, the amount in existence being inflated and deflated like a concertina.

It would seem that, as a start, a simple index based, for example, in the first instance on the average cost of living for a skilled artisan's household would serve. It would be the duty of impartial statisticians studying the tendencies to advise from time to time if the index could be, in general, improved and made more representative. It seems in every way desirable, in order to avoid any initial unsettling orgy of gambling, to stabilize the index number of prices at the existing level. Whatever that was, an average weekly or yearly budget would be constructed representing, at that time, the chief items, separately, in the cost of living of the type of family chosen as typical. At any future time, the same items in the same quantities as then computed, if again computed at the new prices prevailing, should amount to the same total, however much they might differ individually among themselves, if the price-level does not change.

The Statistical Bureau

This illustrates the principle, though of course in practice the actual work of the statistical bureau contemplated should cover the whole range of the nation's economic activities. One of its functions should be not only to collect but to interpret data, and to answer specific inquiries, not only for the Government but also for all representative bodies carrying on the economic work of the community. It should certainly not be a Government Department any more than the Law or the Universities are, or under any one of them, and especially not under the Treasury. That would be a fatal mistake, as the Treasury would be the one department directly interested in the profits of the issue of new money. The temptation to issue too much and swindle creditors would then always be present. The new money must not be issued with the object of providing a source of revenue for the relief of the taxpayer, though that is the necessary consequence.

The statistical bureau should be nominally directly under the Crown or the supreme head of the State, whoever that may be, and in much the same position, as a disinterested advisory body charged with definite metrological functions, as the National Physical Laboratory. Its recommendations should go formally to Parliament and be normally acted on automatically.

A Reconstituted Mint

For the actual issue of the national money, the Mint should be reconstituted to cover not only coinage but paper money also. The issues would be handed over to the Treasury, and added to the sums levied by taxation. As we have seen, the issue of credit money is really a forced levy or tax on the community, and the money itself is the receipt that the owner has rendered up equivalent value for it, and is entitled to the same value back on demand. The money should bear the legend "Value Received" instead of "Promise to Pay" and also the statement that it is legal tender in the country of issue. It should be regarded by the public as issued to postpone payments they would otherwise be called on to pay by taxes, and they should understand that, if there is at any time too much issued, it will be withdrawn in part by imposing the postponed taxation and destroying the requisite amount of money to prevent the value of the rest falling below par. Money would then appear publicly for the first time in its true light as a permanent floating non-interest bearing debt or liability of the whole community to its owners, repayable in goods and services on demand by mutual exchange within the community.

Criticism of Proposals to Nationalize "Banking"

Apart from initial and transition stages in which it may and probably will be necessary to continue existing credits to producers until such time as they can free themselves from debt – as they quickly would do under an honest monetary system – what the nation needs is not more credits to producers but more money for consumers, and the correct way of issuing this is as a relief to the taxpayers in general. The proposals of the Socialists to nationalize banking show no understanding even of how to operate the system so as to secure a stable internal pricelevel which is the *sine qua non* of any real advance to just economic prosperity. They seem to contemplate doing precisely what the banks are doing now, at ruinous ultimate cost to the industries of the nation, the only difference being that the profits would be devoted to their ameliorative and charitable efforts. It will, of course, be argued that the profits of the issue of new money would be given to assist enterprises *really* beneficial to the public. But this, with the necessity of their being either competitive or forms of government patronage, is a contradiction in terms. They will be given to whom the government really thinks fit, and that, to be sure, is to assist themselves first and all the time, just as it is now given to and through the Bank of England!

Socialists never seem conscious that the people themselves are a better judge of what they need than any government they have ever in past history had, or in the future are likely to get. The whole structure of ameliorations and charities, in which the needy are provided out of what the general taxpayer may be forced to provide, would fall to the ground, like a pack of cards, if everybody had the opportunity of providing out of his own earnings sufficient and to spare for his needs.

Prevention Better than Cure

Prevention is better than cure and the world is being kept diseased by those who wish it worse, so as to have the opportunity of curing it. That is the most amazing feature of the world today. Things go wrong and, ever after, it is saddled with vested interests in the cure. The whole modern bureaucracy is engaged in the consequences of quite elementary and easily comprehended mistakes and it is the most unpopular thing in the world to imply that human beings are really far more able to take care of themselves than left to those by whom their ailments are being nursed. The amount of unemployment that would result from preventing the known errors that have sent the scientific civilization off the rails is appalling to contemplate. It would involve most of the people now trying to sell us things having to give their services to producing them, and most of those who derive their livelihood from busying themselves with the affairs of State having to take a leisurely interest in their own. It is old as the hills, the Hippocratic wisdom of cure opposed to the Aesculapian cultivation of health, now become universal; in brief, quackery *versus* knowledge. Release in fountains of life and leisure the flood of energy that the technologist has now under control, and the world would quickly cure itself of the weeds that thrive in its starved soil.

Interest on Debts

Although the accumulating burden of debt of individualistic societies lies outside in a narrow sense, the subject is so linked with it and is so vital to the future of these societies that it cannot be ignored. The physical explanation is the very much greater amount of labour that has to be expended on the tools or plant required to operate power production than in primitive methods. The enormous capacity of modern prime-movers enables production to be achieved on a corresponding scale, but at the same time make the provision of the necessary plant quite outside the capacity of individuals to provide. Hence arose the joint stock company by which the savings of large numbers of people could be used in a single enterprise.

In no sphere is there such a total inversion of ideas, in changing from an economics of want to an economics of abundance, as in that of interest on debts.

In the first place it would be completely mistaken to suppose that there is any physical basis for the so-called laws of interest, simple and compound. The first law applies when the interest is periodically paid, and the second when it is not paid but accumulates, itself bearing interest. These laws are in origin purely mathematical. Certain assumptions are made and the consequences quantitatively worked out. That is all. What exactly these assumptions amount to, beyond the agreement of one individual to pay another so much a year interest for the use of so much principal, it would puzzle anyone to say. They are purely arbitrary and conventional agreements without any necessary physical justification at all. Such justification as is offered for interest is usually a vague biological rather than physical one, along the lines of the increment accruing in agriculture, each seed bringing forth thirty-, sixty-, or even a hundred-fold. But it is perfectly open to anyone now to challenge the theoretical basis of interest. In practice, however, there is no reason why anyone should himself abstain from consuming in order to lend to another unless he derives some advantage from it. However, as we have seen, unless individuals wish to trust their grey-hairs to be supported by the benevolence of governments, they are bound to try to save in the hey-day of their powers. Usually there are many similar reasons, such as to provide for the better education of their children when they are arriving at maturity, and to insure against accidents, which are sufficiently compelling, even without the inducement of increment. The dawning realization of this is responsible for many suggested reforms.

If Increment Looking Forward then Decrement looking Backward

A correspondent, Basil Paterson of Edinburgh, submitted to the author during the writing of this book an interesting suggestion that at least indicates how purely arbitrary the conventional mathematical treatment of interest really is. His argument rested on some such consideration as this. Though it be agreed to pay in one year's time, say, £5 for the use of £100 lent now this is not the same as agreeing to pay another at the end of the second year. Rather the value of the £100 at the end of the first year has to be discounted to its present value £95, now, so that the second years' interest ought to be five per cent of £95 and so on. And who shall deny him? It seems to give the money-lender a little of his own medicine. He works out that the consequence of this would be to reduce the Compound Interest law to the same as the present Simple Interest law. For the latter, taking the above illustration, and expressing the interest as a fraction instead of a percentage, the successive yearly interest payments would be one twentieth, one twenty-first, one twenty-second, one twenty-third, one twenty-fourth, and so one, becoming one hundredth or one per cent after eighty years. One of the applications claimed is in the pawnbroking business, where the least rate of interest profitable becomes usurious if extended for any length of time, and which the above method of estimation would tend to correct.

Paterson's Interest Law
Discounting the Principal

It is of interest to apply the higher mathematics to the foregoing idea, and consider, instead of the increment accruing step by step by yearly intervals, an infinite number of infinitesimal periods, so as to make the process continuous instead of being supposed to occur by yearly steps. This does not affect the result that the Compound Interest law is thus reduced to the ordinary Simple Interest law, but we so arrive at one very simple result for the law of simple interest itself. Under these circumstances, as the time is indefinitely increased without limit, the total interest accruing becomes nearer and nearer to the principal in amount and can never exceed it however long the loan lasts. The mathematical formula applying to this case is

$$iT = -230\ 26\ [log_{10}(1 - f)]$$

where i is the rate of interest per cent per annum, T the time in years, and f the fraction of the principal accruing as interest. From this and

Table of Simple Interest (New Law) for £100 Principal

Years multiplied by rate % p.a.	Total Interest (New Law)			Saving to Debtor (as compared with Old Law)		
	£	s.	d.	£	s.	d.
1		19	11			1
2	1	19	7			5
3	2	19	1			11
4	3	18	5		1	7
5	4	17	6		2	6
6	5	16	6		3	6
8	7	13	9		6	3
10	9	10	4		9	8
15	13	18	7	1	1	5
20	18	2	6	1	17	6
25	22	2	5	2	17	7
50	39	6	11	10	13	1
100	63	4	5	36	15	7
184'14	86	2	10	100	0	0
200	86	9	4	113	10	8
1000	99	19	11	900	0	1

a table of logarithms the new interest table can readily be constructed. In the one above, the interest accruing per £100 of principal is shown in the middle column, the time in years multiplied by the rate of interest per cent per annum in the first column, and the saving to the debtor by the new method of calculation in the last column.

The above makes it clear that though for low rates of interest and short periods there is little difference, for high rates and long periods the difference is enormous. The originator of the scheme pointed out that its obvious objection is that it encourages the investor to draw out and re-invest his money every year, but that is completely impossible with permanent long term and non-redeemable loans such as the national debt. If applied to these it would probably suffice instead of the simple redemption scheme later referred to. An alternative way would be to continue the interest payments at the ordinary rate, regarding the difference (shown above in the last column) as a sinking fund repayment. In this mode of reckoning the payments would be made at uniform rate as now for a limited time and then stop. This time is given under this law as one hundred and eighty-four and one-seventh years divided by the rate of interest per cent per annum, as indicated in the above table.

Gesell's Ideas of Making Money Itself Depreciate

A much more sweeping proposal is that of the money reformer, Silvio Gesell, who would make all money depreciate with time, say five per cent per annum, or a penny in the pound per month. It would only be maintained current as legal tender by periodically stamping it like an insurance card. If the public would stand this, and they seem positively to love this sort of government edict, it certainly would have some remarkable consequences. It is claimed that it would, as it were, shift down the whole scale of interest by five per cent bodily, in the sense that where now we should have to pay four per cent for a loan, then we should get one per cent for taking the money off the owner's hands and saving him the five per cent deterioration. If so, all borrowing for government and municipal public works would be done at a one per cent profit rather than at a four per cent interest rate. The scheme is actually being advocated by one British Chamber of Commerce and is likely to prove exceedingly popular in municipal, if not government, circles. Gesell's original idea was to prevent anyone hoarding money, to increase its "velocity of circulation", and compel people who had it to spend it quickly. But the possibility at least of this effect of changing the basis or datum-line from which increment is reckoned, from zero to a five per cent decrement, is worth independent consideration, as all the other results would equally well be secured if money were issued nationally as described without making it rot or depreciate.

Objections

The view taken in this book is that money is a binding contract between the owner who has given up for nothing, not even for interest payment, the use of goods and services to the community and in common justice he ought to receive back just as much as he has given up. Stamping the money with a five per cent per annum tax would bring in a revenue to the community sir iilar to what it would get if, instead of a bank-rate of, say, five per cent on the issue, the nation issued the money in exchange for national debt securities destroyed, or in lieu of this charged five per cent to the existing borrowers instead of the banks. This is not to deny that the nation could do both, that is to say, itself take the profits of the issue now appropriated by the banks and then charge a five per cent per annum maintenance tax or stamp-duty to keep the money current. But there really does seem no justification at all for taxing the medium of exchange, and though it may be difficult at first sight to devise means for dodging the payment, it certainly would create a powerful stimulus to the inventive mind to try so to do. In this respect it seems calculated to produce exactly the opposite effect to what is intended. People would try to refuse to accept it just as powerfully as they would be constrained to spend it, and although, admittedly, it might put them to some trouble, the inducement to use money as little as possible, and to enter into mutual understandings to this end, would be as great as the inducement to spend it as soon as they received it. Whereas, on the plan here advocated, hoarding simply would not matter, for it has the effect, as has been shown, of postponing indefinitely the payment of taxation, as more money would be issued to make up for increase of hoarding if it occurred. Also, instead of making money still more of a hectic source of anxiety and hurry, the plan here favoured would make credit money an invaluable social device for freeing men from artificial financial and attendant worries and the inverted illusions about money fostered by the present system.

The Possibility of Arbitrarily lowering Interest Rates

The possibility, not to say desirability, of shifting the datum-line from which increment is reckoned to one below zero, so as to start with an initial decrement, does not seem to be against, but rather in keeping with, the, at bottom, purely arbitrary character of interest in an age of potential abundance. Quite broadly, as in the day of scarcity, when the importance of increasing production was paramount, the banking system in effect shifted the datum-line from nothing to five per cent or so above zero by issuing money as a debt to themselves, now that the emphasis is on increasing consumption there seems nothing impracticable in devising means for lowering it below zero, by putting a tax or impost upon being in possession of it. In the one case, people owing it had to pay five per cent per annum to bring it into existence and, in the other, people owning it have to pay five per cent per annum to prevent it going out of existence!

The Probable Effect in Increasing Capital Indebtedness

But one further comment on this aspect of the Gesell scheme may be made.

Although there seems no reason to doubt it would now have some effect at least in lowering the general rate of interest it is not so clear what the relative effect would be as regards nonproductive indebtedness (either old debts or new ones) and productive capital. At first sight it would seem that it ought to lead to rapid repayment of existing debts, so far as the terms of the bond permitted, by purchase with existing money to escape the tax, and their replacement by non-interest bearing or even lightly taxed debts. But, in the case of productive capital, money is merely an intermediary, and productive capital yields a revenue of real wealth which cannot be so easily redistributed by taxation, as the effect of so-called socialistic legislation of the last half-century abundantly makes clear. It would appear therefore that, the fund available for investment being limited, astute people would subscribe for productive enterprises rather than towards non-productive expenditure, that is for "industrials" rather than government and municipal bonds. Although this should lead to a lowering of the rate of interest on new money invested in industry it would be at the expense of a corresponding appreciation of the capital values as regards existing indebtedness. As regards the non-productive class of loans, if not redeemable they should probably also appreciate in exchange-value, and, to a lesser extent, if redeemable. "O! what a tangled web we weave when first we practise to deceive." Is this really the sort of monetary policy necessary in, or worthy of, a great scientific age?

Straightforward Debt Redemption by Taxation

The author's plan for reducing the burden of debt is quite straightforward. It is to earmark the tax levied on what used to be termed "unearned income", or the part derived from savings, for the purchase of the investment, and the revenue from the part so acquired for the same purpose. The effect of this is to make all debts terminable by amortization. It is convenient to express the time required for complete amortization in units of time in which the principal returns the interest. That is, the unit of time is 100 divided by i, where i is the rate of interest per cent per annum – twenty years for a five per cent, twenty-five years for a four per cent investment, and so on. In these units, the times for various rates of income-tax are as follows:—

Rate of Tax: the pound.	6/ –	5/ –	4/ –	3/ –	2/ –	1/ – in
Units of Time:	1'73	1'84	2'01	2'23	2'56	3'29

As an example, taking the 4s. in the pound rate of tax, the time would be 40'2 years for an investment yielding five per cent and 50'25 years for one yielding four per cent per annum. At this rate of tax, about three-fourths of the redemption is effected by interest payments on the part already redeemed and only one-fourth by taxation.

In this way the productive capital wealth of the nation in the sense defined would automatically become the property of the nation after having returned to the owner interest varying from 1'73 times the principal for a 6s. rate of taxation to 3'29 times for a IS rate. It may be called compound redemption, in that the interest on the part already acquired is not used for national expenditure but "saved" to purchase the principal. For non-productive capital debts of the nature of the national debt, for which simple rather than compound redemption would be more natural, the time required is of course much longer, being, for half-redemption, about seventy years for a 4s. tax-rate and a five per cent investment. As the quantity of debt unredeemed is reduced, the rate of redemption is proportionately slower, so that, theoretically, it is always approaching but never reaching nothing. In the above illustration one per cent would be unredeemed after four hundred and sixty years. In many respects the suggestion of Paterson already discussed is superior for the amortization of this class of non-productive permanent debt.

The Nationalization of Capital is National "Saving"

The main advantages claimed for the scheme are that it would be in accord with the physical decrement of accumulated capital wealth, and enable obsolete and obsolescent plant to be kept up to date by private enterprise. But in the future, when the existing debt was cleared off, a revenue would accrue to the nation from the ownership of the capital which could then be used to furnish national dividends to the nation. It need not be discussed here further except to call attention to its novel feature as compared with other so-called political nationalization schemes, which in effect do not vest the ownership of capital in the nation but merely redistribute it among individual owners, merely multiplying task-masters. This is because the nation is also "saving" instead of just spending its revenue from taxation.

It will be asked how the Chancellor of the Exchequer is to provide for the National Expenditure if so large a part of the taxes is taken for Capital Redemption, and the answer is from the sources now used to demoralize the community by ameliorative legislation. Almost from the moment the new monetary system was started, unemployment would cease, except in so far as the really unemployable were concerned, and there would be a great progressive expansion in the revenue of real wealth produced, with corresponding increase in the total proceeds of taxation if the rate remained unchanged. In addition, instead of all the capital depreciating with old age and new inventions and improvements being blocked from application by the accumulation of these colossal irrepayable debts, the proceeds from the redemption would be returned to the production system and be available for keeping the whole economic organization up to date, replacing obsolescent and outworn buildings and plant and employing the latest and most time-saving methods of production. In this the nation as the owner of an ever-increasing part of the capital through the redemption scheme would benefit no less than the individuals who supplied it by abstinence from their own consumption in the first instance.

CHAPTER VIII

THE PRACTICAL SITUATION

IS the New or the Old Economics upside Down?

In this book the critical exposure has been attempted of the chief errors of the past. A civilization of truly unlimited promise has been side-tracked from the broad highway of progress and plunged into a morass of bottomless deceit and evasion, in which it is now aimlessly floundering and struggling, and from which it is doubtful whether it will ever again emerge. If it has been necessary so much to reinforce the cold impersonal language of science by the denunciation of fraudulent practices, it is because delays are dangerous and these practices ought by now to be well-known to all men of good-will anxious to avoid another holocaust.

We began our inquiries by asking the ordinary man to reverse his natural way of looking upon his own money and to consider how he got it (it being nothing for something), rather than its subsequent use to him, in which he merely gets back what was given up for it. Once men will think in that way then money itself begins to appear as the opposite of what it is supposed to be, which is the going without of a vast collection of useful and valuable property by the community fully entitled to own it, and which any individual is at liberty to own if desired, though in fact only by getting another to take his place in going without it.

At first, no doubt, all these ideas appear upside down, a merely pedantic and wilful inversion of the natural way of looking at the problem. But it is safe to say that anyone who has ever really started on this road and tried to follow it can never go back. Nothing in the whole world can ever look quite the same again. Is it the new view that is upside down or the old? Those queues of hopeless and miserably nourished unemployed which, if stretched out in single rank, shoulder to shoulder, would line the motor-road from Lands End to John o' Groats and be jammed together to get them all in—are they a sign of poverty or wealth? Those columns and columns of stock-exchange securities that daily sprawl over the pages of the morning newspapers – are they really evidence of national prosperity? The national debt alone, some £8,000 millions, or £160 per man, woman, or child, bringing in something like a million of interest every day to someone, is it debt or wealth? Everything depends on the point of view. If we would understand national economic problems we must drop our conventional ideas altogether and turn ourselves right round, just as we had to do with money itself in order to see it in its true light.

Abundance First, Apportionment Second

Then again how utterly inverted appears the ordinary mentality derived from the past age of scarcity that there is only a limited amount of wealth in the world and what anyone gets is at the expense of someone else, and all the jealous bickering over the share of the conflicting interests in the output, rather than a common and loyal co-operation

to make the output larger, and provide and distribute more
with less work. As regards any one moment of time it is, of
course, true that there is only so much available for
distribution and no more, but in the sense intended it is
about as true as if every shell fired in the War had been
regarded as one less left to fire, and totally untrue. Wealth
is a flow, not a store, and just as during the war the output
of munitions rose steadily the longer the war lasted, so in
peace the output of the things consumed and used in living
could, but for the monetary stranglehold, be continuously
increased to any extent desired in reason. As it is, on the
average, probably not one person in five is doing anything
whatever to produce or assist others to produce what is
being consumed, and the whole productive work is carried
on by a small minority. The rest of the gainfully-employed
population is either engaged in bargaining as to the price
and trying to sell the product to people with insufficient
money to buy, or actually deriving a livelihood by
obstructing and hindering production. So it is in the
international sphere; fiscal entanglements of every kind are
erected to prevent the smooth exchange of the abundance
of one nation with that of another.

The Attitude of the Public Towards Cost

If there is one sphere in which a change of heart is called
for, it is in the attitude of the public towards costs, and their
misguided passion for cheapness. This attitude is of course
induced by the artificial scarcity of money, but what does it
end in? Far more is being spent nowadays on selling things
than in making them. Although everyone wants to be paid
well for his work, and price is nothing else but the sum total
of the payments made from the moment production starts

until the sale is effected, as soon as people turn from earning money to spending it, they all with one accord want to beat down the price, and, like the bankers, want to get something for nothing. They finish up by paying on the average probably twice as much as they need do and reduce their own earnings to half as much as they might be, three-quarters of the cost representing unnecessary costs of commercial haggling and bargaining, competitive sales organization, and advertising, which do not contribute an iota to the value received. The cost of distributing the product ought, like the cost of producing it, to be exactly known and to be brought down to the minimum by efficient organization, not raised to the maximum by wasteful and unnecessary competition. Even more could be done to raise the general standard of living, and give all a larger income and greater leisure, by deflecting into production an increasing proportion of those now engaged in distribution and selling, than by the full and efficient employment of all existing labour and capital. Hours of labour and rates of wages and salary are purely traditional. The eight-hour day which seemed so outrageous a demand to the Victorian taskmasters is already considered a maximum rather than a minimum. Free the workers from the competition of backward and less civilized workers by freeing the exchanges, and provide money automatically sufficient to distribute at the actual competitive price all the goods and services the production system is actually turning out, and the whole nation could live on a much ampler scale and with far less work than now. It is idle to give estimates which are but guesses, though a five-fold increase of income with much shorter working hours, as quoted by some of the technocrats in America, seems in Europe to be not unreasonably within sight even of people now alive. But it is far better to give people sufficient money resources to cultivate their own personal lives and tastes according to their own choice than to professionalize recreation, education, and culture and make them a source of commercial profit.

Government Interference in Economics not Helpful

There are many who may disagree with the author's view that, if money were freed from its stranglehold on the creative functions of society and restored to its proper place as a distributory mechanism, and if, by amortization or otherwise, the unlimited accumulation of communal debt was prevented, and that already accumulated reduced, there is not much wrong with the productive economic system as such. All sorts of fears will no doubt be entertained as to the consequences, but in the author's opinion none of the problems likely to arise will *then* be difficult to deal with, as and if they occur. An economic system is necessarily an equilibrium condition integrating the actions of the individuals comprising it, and the result cannot help being an average of all the efforts exerted by the individuals in providing most efficiently and least wastefully for their own personal livelihood. With a better physical understanding of the national aspects, and of the conventions underlying the economics of individuals, less and less interference from Government and more and more intelligent direction from those within the system itself, actively engaged in the work of supplying and satisfying the economic needs of the community, seem called for. If too many people try to "save" the rate of interest will fall and make it less advantageous to do so, and if saving is insufficient to maintain and increase the productive capital, the rate of interest will rise to counteract the tendency. In an Age of

Plenty these matters can safely be left to adjust themselves, once the monetary and debt system has been put into accord with physical reality. It is the creation of money for speculative gambling that distorts this truth.

A Progressive Evolution of Industry

This is not to deny the need or importance of a progressive evolution of industry from its present bondage to ownership, and from the last vestige of economic subservience or slavery. To this end the plans of the Guild-Socialists are directed. The bitter struggles of the past century will not have been in vain if thereby they have developed among the personnel and rank-and-file of labour a loyalty and sense of responsibility to themselves which they should be proud to devote to the work of the whole community. But these further advances all depend on a gradual and orderly growth, which, in the first instance, can only come about through a rising standard of living. This is being held back and frustrated by the perpetual strife and sabotage that have marked the struggles of the past, and which are primarily due to our utterly fraudulent monetary system. The same could be said of all the ameliorative social legislation of the past century, which merely tried to deal with and diminish the suffering occasioned by the money system without in one single instance intelligently striking at the cause. But all these social and political problems lie without the proper scope of this book, the primary object of which has been to expound the legitimate role of money, to deal faithfully with the existing system as it has grown up, and to show how it is frustrating every effort towards bringing about a saner and happier state of things. Whatever further social changes experience may dictate, no unbiassed inquirer into the subject of money today can long escape the conclusion that, until the system is drastically transformed and its mistakes eliminated, there can be no hope of peace, honesty, or stability again in this world.

Monetary Reform First

However desirable and necessary it may be to overhaul the political, social, and economic machinery of the modern State to allow scope and freedom for the new possibilities of life introduced by modern scientific progress to develop, the peculiar difficulties that have attended this progress are not due in any direct way to its obstruction by old habits of thought but by the new and totally false ideas concerning money. It is necessary in this respect to return to the fundamental basis of money as something no private person should be allowed to create for himself. All, equally, should have to give up for money the equivalent value in goods and services before they can obtain it. What we have now is not properly speaking a monetary system at all, and money today, as something always being created and destroyed by borrowing and repayment, is a phenomenon new in history. So also are all the familiar evils of the day new in history. They are all consequences of a false money system. The continual growth of unemployment is an example. The power of employment is not given ultimately by possession of money but by possession of the physical necessities used and consumed by the worker in the course of his employment. Instead of these being only obtainable by people who have themselves given up equivalent goods or services, the nation's stock of its means of employment is continually being depleted by defalcations only different from the petty peculations of the counterfeiter and forger of notes on account of their universality and colossal extent. Modern unemployment, like modern money, is a new phenomenon. No person who really understands the physical significance of what is going on in the economic world today, through the arbitrary private creation and destruction of money, can feel any surprise whatever that the world has been brought so nearly to disaster.

Even a schoolboy can understand the distinction between lending to another, that is going without oneself, and lending what belongs to someone else, so avoiding having to go without oneself. Economists still write as though the nation existed for the sake of banks, the public being adequately compensated by the banks not charging their ordinary clients and customers for their services in keeping their accounts. But surely the banks are hardly the people to be trusted to advise as to the economic aflfairs of a great commercial and industrial nation. The ordinary man at least will appreciate the importance of honesty in the monetary system, though he is likely greatly to overestimate the difficulties in the way of the nation getting it.

The Existing System on the Horns of a Dilemma

By those fundamentally opposed to any reform, which would stabilize the internal price-level and prevent the incessant fluctuation in the value of money out of which they derive their livelihood by some form of peculation, the issue has so far been represented as an alternative between fixing the internal price-level or fixing the foreign exchanges. The real truth is, rather, that these interests want the banks to continue to be able to create money, for their own and similar uses, without having to bother about finding genuine lenders. They want a certain predictable initial rise of prices, with the exchanges fixed or pegged to bring back the value again to par *after* prices have been raised. They want the banks, who provide them with money for nothing, to destroy it after they have profited by the use of it. But if the first were prevented, the question of the exchanges would assume very much less importance.

True, if banks are to continue to be at liberty to raise the internal price-level by fictitious loans and, if this is not periodically brought down again by devious methods adopted to fix the exchanges, all our imports will cost us proportionately more, just as the value of the home money is debased, and our investments abroad will thereby be proportionately reduced in value both as regards principal and interest. The opposite of course applies to the present time. The monetary policies adopted to benefit the rentier at home operate as much against foreign as against home-debtors and are proving a powerful disintegrating influence within the Empire. This nation has only itself to blame if its foreign debtors go bankrupt or find other means of evading their artificially inflated burdens altogether.

The common argument in favour of pegging the exchanges is that the nation's food, which it buys so largely from abroad with the interest payment of past investments, will otherwise be jeopardized. But as an argument against the nation issuing its own money it is ludicrous. It is the existing system which is perpetually on the horns of a dilemma, and at its wits' end how to monkey with the internal price-level without jeopardizing foreign investments. Prevent the first and the second will not occur.

The Economic Necessity of Frontiers

Nevertheless there will still remain very powerful interests in favour of fixing the exchanges rather than the internal price-level. They will have thought it out this way. When the exchanges are free, they go of course against the country in which goods are the dearer to produce and in favour of those in which they are cheaper, so preventing the markets of the former from being subjected to the competition of the latter. The money as it crosses the frontier then adjusts itself automatically to the costs of living in the new country. If they are lower there the money loses in buying power and, if higher, it gains, so that it is always able to buy much the same wealth, whichever side of the frontier it is. But on the ordinary financial and pecuniary principles of the rentier and banker this appears wrong, and it ought, they think, to be corrected by some way of fixing the exchanges. It seems absurd that a person in possession of a fixed monetary income, crossing a frontier from where goods are dear and the standard of living and wages high, should be no better off than he was before he emigrated to a country where goods are cheap and the standard of living and wage-level are low.

The argument really amounts to this. That a person who has saved in one country and has a definite income should be able to transfer himself to another country and spend his income where he can get most for it – that he should be able to earn it in the highest and spend it in the lowest market. Frontiers, which are a protection to those who have to earn their living, are a hindrance to those who do not. All the propaganda towards the unification of the whole world in one brotherhood, when they are all still at different stages of evolution and standards of living, though no doubt arising from falsely idealistic religious sentiment, is sedulously fostered by those who do not have to earn their living, or, if they do, wish to spend what they earn in another country. The difference between leaving the exchanges free and attempting to stabilize them is that, while no impediment is offered to those who wish to reside in a foreign country, there is no economic advantage to be gained by it. Whereas if the exchanges are fixed, then clearly it is quite unnecessary to emigrate to get the advantage in spending of a lower standard of living elsewhere. It does not matter whether they are fixed "automatically" by a gold-standard or, as appears to have been also the case in the 1929 U.S.A. slump, by arbitrary deflation, the standard of wages and living in the more advanced countries is thereby depressed to that of the standard prevailing in the less advanced countries.

Free Exchanges Mean Free Trade

With free foreign exchanges there would be no need of tariff barriers or complicated fiscal agreements, the nations would be free to trade for their mutual benefit, and there would be no such thing as the general standards of living in the more developed being endangered by external competition with the rest of the world. Genuine lending and borrowing between nations would cease to be a danger and become unobjectionable if internal price-levels were fixed and the exchanges freed. In brief, the whole complicated fiscal paraphernalia that now hinders goods from crossing frontiers could disappear if the monies of different countries were only able to exchange at their respective purchasing powers each in its own country, and if the arbitrary parity ratios established when they were all convertible into gold were abandoned once for all. The pricelevel in any one country being fixed as described, variations in the foreign exchanges would then be almost entirely due to variations in the price-levels abroad, and this, surely, is as it should be.

Compromise Hardly Feasible

Many influential people, if only because they object to sudden changes, will wish to compromise by continuing the banking system with such modifications and safeguards as the modern philosophy of money can suggest. But it is not in the nature of science to believe false accountancy to be a matter for compromise. Some people must gain to others' hurt, and the whole argument in favour of compromise is really directed towards ascertaining exactly how the injuries can best be concealed from the knowledge of the unsuspecting victims.

Clearly the vital point on which no compromise is possible is the aggregate quantity of money, which ought always to be publicly known, as was recognized for the ancient token money that circulated in Athens and Sparta many centuries before Christ. The power of increasing or decreasing this aggregate quantity of money must be wrested from the banking system and vested in the central control of the nation. Moreover, the last people to trust in deciding whether the issue should be increased or decreased are those born and brought up in the jargon of the money-market. All their cant phrases–"speculative boom", "fictitious prosperity", "over confidence", and the like, so glibly swallowed by supposed impartial students of money in the past, should be now universally recognized as the polite way of informing the initiated that the standard of living of the working class is rising dangerously above subsistence level, and the appropriate monkeying with the quantity of money is being engineered to bring it down.

CHAPTER IX

HONESTY THE BEST MONETARY POLICY

THE Signs of a New Truth

Our task would not be complete if this book failed to convey some hint at least to the mind of the reader of the signs, at first often slight but cumulative and interwoven, by which a scientific investigator or pioneer into novel regions of thought knows when he is on sure ground, even when everyone else may think him mad. This is a philosophic question of great interest, for, if we examine the history of progress, the direction it has taken appears so often a matter of intuition and conviction, rather than to depend on anything that at the time would have been accepted as convincing or logical proof. Yet this is perhaps an external or mass judgment of those who, consciously or not, accept as proof subsequent practical experience rather than fundamental theoretical principles.

One, certainly, of these signs is how what appears nothing so much as a jig-saw puzzle of disconnected events and conundrums suddenly seems to fit together into a picture, to be lost again in a haze of uncertainty, but always returning, each time a little more orderly and definite.

Something of this must have happened to many who, once having started on the road of reversing the conventional illusions, induced by the substitution of money for wealth, can never turn back until they have restored concrete reality and physical ideas everywhere to their rightful place, and can never again hold the conventional and impressionistic beliefs, still prevalent today as to the cause and cure of the world's unrest. There appears a satisfying correspondence between the whole nature of the unsolved problem and the dawning interpretation of it, such as that not one of the maladies afflicting the relations of men today are due to any real physical insufficiency, such as characterized the earlier epochs of history. They are due to the exact opposite, 'over-production,'' glut,' competition for markets, and the like, which renders the continued existence of poverty and destitution a physical absurdity. Where Mr. Baldwin asked "What is the use of being able to make goods if you cannot sell them?" the new economist would say at once "Why dhnnot we sell them? What is money for?" and so cut at once the Gordian knot of the whole tangle.

Another sign is the projection of the new view back into the past, and how, there also, it throws light upon what before was mysterious and inexplicable. In this connection it is a gratifying sign that many modem students of history are beginning to realize the important part played by monetary causes in the changes of fortune and direction that have overtaken nations. They are now comprehending that these monetary causes give a far truer interpretation of the real ferment at work than the personalities and motives of those who were apparently the principal actors in the drama. In the history of the past century we have had occasion to notice how the gold-standard has been operating, and how it has been completely unable to limit, as it was intended, the effect of a false monetary system to each individual country, but gradually extending and widening the area of disturbance until it now embroils the whole world.

Another sign of the power of a new and true idea is its extension from its immediate application to throw new light upon cognate problems. Thus we have seen that the identical mistake which explains the failure of the money system explains also the old confusions in the political and economic sphere concerning capital, and the chronic struggle, as much now as ever in doubt as to the issue, between what is termed capitalism or individualism and socialism.

These then are some of the channels through which a new idea makes its way into the general mind in spite of its being in opposition to inherited and stereotyped habits of thought, and it is the significant glory of our age that owing to the general quickening in the pace of life, to wider and more liberal education, not only of the formal type, but in the very atmosphere a modern citizen breathes, this period of incubation is becoming incredibly shortened. So that, whereas it took three or four generations, a century ago, for anything new in thought to permeate the general mind, today we see the whole process going on before our eyes from year to year. Once the fundamental fact is grasped that we are living in an age distinguished only by its science and by its understanding and control of the physical realities of the external world, then, surely, we must accept the corollary that anything setting itself up against physical reality cannot be allowed to continue. Any attempt to order the world along a physically impassable road is contrary to the motive power behind progress and, if persisted in, can only bring disaster. In brief, we live in a scientific age, the purpose of which is frustrated by the survival of beliefs in money, as the practical mechanism of distribution, which are the exact opposite of those which have made that age possible. The symptoms and repercussions are of infinite obscurity and complexity, but the remedy is neither obscure nor complex. It is as devastatingly simple and effective as correcting an error of arithmetic.

Monetary Reform Begins at Home.
The U.S.A. Plan

Many people wish to make money reform an international question, and have the vague idea that money ought to be international. Some of the interests in favour of this, those who wish to be able to earn on the highest and spend in the lowest market, have just been referred to. Others believe that until the international banker is under control it is idle to attempt to deal with the internal monetary system. Many think President Roosevelt's policy is really directed to a trial of strength with the international monetary interests before dealing with those nearer home. Whatever may be thought of it, it does not seem as yet to contain a single clear principle which, in the author's view, is essential to any true permanent reform. The national expenditure on economic reconstruction in America is on a scale that will saddle the United States with a permanent new debt, involving it in an increase of taxation to the extent of something like an additional £100 millions a year.

Now it is quite a mistake to imagine that there is likely to be anything at all antagonistic to the monetary interests in a policy designed to increase national debt, for that, in the end, is the chief object and purpose nowadays of war itself. However it may be superficially criticized as extravagant, it is right in the main line of least resistance of the old system. The object of that system is the increase of all the forms of national debt. The acid test of reform is their redemption or amortization out of the revenue. It all would have been totally unnecessary, if the American nation had taken the only sure step to ultimate success from the first, instead of postponing it and perhaps never reaching it. The first step is to deal with the issue of money itself. For the power of both international and internal banking alike depend on the ability to keep the internal price-level always on the move. Put that under statistical national control, by making all money national and regulating the aggregate amount issued, and free the foreign exchanges, and a nation with an honest monetary system has nothing to fear from the manipulation of the price-level in other countries. But leave the money at home dishonest and allow its price-level to be varied by creating and destroying it as required for speculators, and, sooner or later, it will be made the certain victim of external attack designed to reduce its standard of living to the lowest prevailing elsewhere.

In this respect the United States is certainly stronger and better able to protect itself than the older and more debt-ridden nations of Europe. It may be, as all sensible men must hope, that the courageous positive steps taken by the President of the United States to defeat the artificial paralysis of its economic system by the banking system will leave him strong and respected enough politically to do something likely to be more permanently effective than anything he has yet attempted, that he will be able, in fact, to give the world a money system based on physical reality. But this still appears to be very much in doubt. If it is argued that speed was the essence of the problem and that quick returns were essential owing to the widespread acute distress, it is just as quick to issue new money correctly as incorrectly, when the principles involved are understood. In any case, the nation had had to assume provisional control over the whole banking system, and under these circumstances, pending complete abolition of the private issue of money, the amount in existence could have been stabilized, and increased by national issues. If this had been done by raising genuine loans and putting them back into circulation by issuing new money with corresponding remission of taxes, the price-level would not have been disturbed. On the other hand, if the object were deliberately to raise prices, no one can pretend there is any difficulty in doing that – the genuine loans would not to that extent have been necessary. The situation from the first moment would then have been absolutely under national control.

Synopsis of the Principles of Reform

However it is done there can be no question what has to be done. Money is a debt which cannot be repaid because there exists nothing with which to repay it, and capital is a debt that cannot be repaid because against it there exists things of social use only, that can never again be converted into what individuals require and consume. With regard to the first, let it be issued by and for the whole nation, as and when goods appear on the market for use and consumption without money and which cannot be sold without forcing down prices. With regard to the second, make all debts redeemable by earmarking part of the revenue they yield for amortization, and, for non-productive permanent debts, calculating the yield to allow for the discounting of the future value of the principal to its value in the present as well as for the increment of that value in the future. Let us have, in the first, physical counters instead of magical zeros below zero, and in the second, if increments looking forwards also decrements looking backwards.

As regards transition stages, fix a price index on the cost of the more important expenses of an average middle-class household, require the banks always to keep pound for pound of national money against their current accounts drawable by cheque, set up a national advisory statistical bureau on an independent scientific basis, and reconstitute the mint for the issue of all money. Avoid as the plague schemes for nationalizing banks. The object is to stop private minting and nationalize money itself, not to control legitimate account-keeping or other financial institutions. In future earmark, on the one hand, the proceeds of the issue of money for the relief of the taxpayer, and on the other the proceeds of taxation on "unearned incomes" for the purchase for the nation of the capital from which they are derived. These at least cover all that appears fundamental and essential as regards the internal reform of the system in the most straightforward and open manner possible, and with the minimum of interference with the nation's economic organization.

Free the Exchanges

As regards its external economic transactions,' both with other nations and with the members of its own family, free the exchanges and put them also under national supervision. Let them find their own level and not drag down nations to the level of the lowest. Let us forget how many dollars in America, francs in France, or marks in Germany used to go to the pound under the gold-standard, and make sure that just as many do go to the pound as will buy the same in the country in question as the pound does here. Reduce gold to

the rank of a commodity merely for convenient
international settlement and let it be bought and sold like
any other goods. Then there is no advantage or
disadvantage in the exchange of one country's money for
another that does not at once correct itself by making it
easier to settle by goods rather than by exchanging money.
Then countries can only lend their own goods and services
and be repaid with those of their debtors. Instead of being
rivals and enemies in each others' markets and setting up
tariff barriers to protect their own, and all alike the dupes of
complicated financial operations in which A lends what B
borrows and C supplies, nations will be protected by their
exchanges, and at long last find peace.

Tall claims? Aye! but the half is not yet said. Let but a
single nation stand forth armed cap-à-pie in the garment of
honesty, and it can face the world without fear of the
chicaneries and conspiracies that still serve for the
monetary systems of other countries. Roosevelt, it would
seem, does not believe it politically, but nevertheless it
would appear to be scientifically true. Reform begins at
home. Let the League of Nations look to this. To try and
reform the whole world without first dealing with the evil
in our midst may be a crusade but it is not practical politics.
But to gird on the sword and buckler of truth would be to
make the whole world our ally, though all outside were still
in the grip of the money-power. As Major Douglas has
wisely said, in the same connection, you do not solve a
problem by making it larger.

The Real Universal Dictatorship

No doubt many will ridicule the idea that such a nursery notion as honest counting is, in these days, the key to problems which have baffled for generations the collective wisdom of the world's statesmen and advisers. But what does the modem world owe to them? It is a world that has been created by just this type of honesty and by the abolition of all pretended miracles, in the realm of physical realities, to the limbo of superstition and magic.

It is a curious thought that the earliest description of the steam-engine in antiquity describes its use for the magic opening of the temple doors, when the priests lit the fires on the altars, to deceive the populace into ascribing to a deity what was the work of the engineer. In much the same way today, the almost boundless fecundity of the creative scientific discoveries and inventions of the age are being appropriated for the purpose of the mysterious opening of doors into the holy of holies of the temples of mammon by a hierarchy of imposters and humbugs, whom it is the first task of a sane civilization to expose and clear out.

Let us have an end of the pretence that economics should not be concerned with morals, for the sort of morality that is in question is one that economics takes as a matter of course, or otherwise there could be no such thing as an economic system at all. The public, if not the economists, after the experience of the war and post-War epoch, are now fully aware of the insidious swindling to which the system of creating and destroying money has lent itself and it should insist on honest money as infinitely more important than honest weights and measures. The "credit-system", which was held up to reverence last century as a great advance in the facilitation of trade and speculation, now appears as a quite childish device for reckoning money from an ever-varying datum-line below the zero, useful no doubt at one time but now coming back to roost.

Thousands of pounds worth of valuable property, which took months to make, pass into the possession of people, who have not contributed a hand's turn to the making by a scratch in a bank-ledger behind the doors of some bank manager's sanctum. Millions of hours of work go into a shipment of goods, perhaps to the other side of the world, and, hi! presto, the exporter is paid for them and given a permit to recoup himself from the goods of his own nation before those he has sold even leave port. Worse, when the foreign goods do arrive to pay for them, the money created disappears. So that under the cabalistic abracadabra of "bills discounted", "acceptances", "money at call and short-notice", the co-existence of nations is becoming an impossibility, and they, too, must go, in order that nothing may hinder the achievement of the physically impossible, the counting below the level where there is anything to count.

Let there be no mistake as to what is wrong. It is not the bill of exchange in itself nor any of the legitimate devices which the commercial world have invented to facilitate international trade, but all banking tricks that could not be performed if the money were made of physical tokens or counters, which cannot be made negative in number. If this were so, then no one whatever, can get money without someone else giving it up, except the State which issues the money in the first instance. The acid test, like the remedy, is really devastatingly simple, but that will not stop it being opposed to the last ditch by the bankers who, while making all sorts of ridiculous claims that they are not continually creating and destroying money by their methods, do not want such claims put to this simple physical test.

Is it so absurd to suggest that the whole complex of the world's madness could and would be cured by replacing the banker by an honest adding machine? That sort of dictatorship already exists universally in fact, whatever the pretence, and the nation that first recognizes the truth will not need to set up any other dictator within its realm nor fear aggression or interference from without.

Reculer Pour Mieux Sauter

Thus we have traced the origin of the present-day social and international unrest, and the frustration of the beneficient scientific advances and inventions which have put at the service of man the primary forces of Nature, to one single cause, to debts that from their nature can never be repaid! Two classes have been distinguished. The first is the debt of goods and services given up when money comes into existence, to replace direct exchange by barter and bridge the time-interval between production and ultimate use or consumption. The second is the capital debt of money given up by individuals, to provide the community with the goods and services required to build up the general productive organization, which are *consumed* in producing the plant and accessories requisite before the initiation of production. These products are of no use to the consumer and by their nature can never be distributed to repay the creditors.

To allay the world's maladies every form of trickery, evasion, and postponement has been tried in vain and many others are proposed, but one remedy remains overlooked, distinguished by directness, simplicity, and effectiveness from all the palliatives, the ameliorations, and the compromises, the blind internecine and international antagonisms and conflicts and the weary round of social and economic strife. It is the truth. Honesty is the best policy, and in no connection could the old adage possibly be more obvious than in regard to money itself. Let us in this respect, as the French say, *reculer pour mieux sauter*. Let us not take a single step forward until we have taken first one back.

Which is it Lawful to Create —Wealth or Money?

Our political, social, and juridical machinery may be outworn and in need of changes of thought and practice to give scope to the new conditions and modes by which men derive their livelihood. Our forms of human association may be moribund, our belief in them shaken, and the spirit of men in eclipse. But these are not causes but consequences. Who dare pretend that it is outside the law and constitution of this or any country to succeed in lightening the labour of living and to enable men to live less like beasts? Or who dare say it is within the law to utter and destroy money?

The monetary system is not outworn or senile. It is novel, upstart, and imperious, defeating technological progress by turning it into the channels of destruction, and challenging the autonomy not of one nation but of all alike, so that now the original authorities constituted for the preservation of that autonomy needs must fawn upon it to rule at all. Hampered by national frontiers, nothing can satisfy it till the whole world is made safe for banking, that its fundamental insolvency may defy exposure. Under the specious guise of a unification of humanity, it aims at absolute dictatorship under which none shall be allowed to live save by its favour and for the advancement of its transcendent whims.

The British Way

Let us not, as other countries have done in the grip of these anti-social innovations, discard a peculiarly native growth, the freedom of the individual and personal life, or be goaded into paroxysms of futile despair under this new absolutism. Let us see it for what it is, deriving its power from the loan of licences to live, its revenues from the tribute that all without exception must pay it, and its irresistible sway from the consequence, only now dawning on a duped world that, its loans being fictitious, its pawn-tickets can never afterwards be redeemed. Let us go back where others have not dared to move, and press forward where they have had to go back. Let us not enslave men that pretenders may rule, but take back our sovereign powers over money in order that men may be free. It is a road Britons have trod before.

The costly system of juridical machinery we maintain to prevent such things happening did not come into existence or grow in public esteem as the hirelings of government, but because of yore it was the bulwark of peoples against the treachery of governments. Though lying for hire be the primrose path to promotion, testing the truth is still the end of law. Even as the heralds of a new Armageddon are taking wing let the truth be tested – within or without the law. To pretend to hear nothing, to know nothing, the organs of public education drugged, the strong in a trap and the wise in a fog – is that too one of the evils of science or the negation of it?

Is the issue to be tested in the Courts or on the hustings? Is it necessary to have a majority to restore a law that has not been revoked, to stop counterfeiting because it has taken everybody in? Is it necessary to break the law to vindicate the law, or trust to democratic organizations, always officered in advance by the very interests they ostensibly oppose? Is it possible to compromise with a lie by inventing new ones to cover up the first? Let us lift back our monetary system on to the narrow gauge of honesty as the first step to a leap forward on the broad gauge of progress. It poisons the very air men breathe, rots them for life or fattens them for death, and imputes its curse to science.

The Real Antagonist

The monetary system is actually based on the very error to the point blank denial of which Western civilization owes its greatness. It serves only the convenience of a parasitic and upstart plutocracy practising a worldly wisdom the exact opposite of that which is the foundation of the age. It prefers the dark in times when all men seek the light, and is sowing the seeds of hatred and war in a world weary to death of strife. It is poisoning the wells of Western civilization, and science must turn from the conquest of Nature to deal with a more sinister antagonist, or lose all it has won.

ENVOI

Clear as crystal waters spring the founts of Truth.
As clear once sprang the science that unloosed
The stream of wealth now dammed and mounting up
To sweep away the age that shuns rebirth.

Virgin springs the fount again, a moment born
Unfouled by intercourse, a moment God
To forge the heart-beat of humanity
And bring belief to being whole and sound.

BIBLIOGRAPHY

1. *Wealth Virtual Wealth and Debt.* F. Soddy. (Allen and Unwin.) 1926. New edition with addition, 1933.

This contains the original ideas of the Energy Theory of Wealth, and the Virtual Wealth Theory of Money, adumbrated in *Cartesian Economics* (Hendersons), 1922, and other pamphlets.

2. *Money versus Man.* F. Soddy. (Elkin Mathews and Marrot.) 1931. A succinct account of the same.

Among books most nearly in line with the above points of view may be mentioned:

3. *The Principal Cause of Unemployment.* Denis W. Maxwell.

(Williams and Norgate.) 1932. 75. 6J.

4. *Promise to Pay*, R. McNair Wilson. (Routledge and Sons.) 1934. Omnia Veritas Ltd, 2014.

(Both of these deal particularly with international trade, the latter claiming, with justice, to make the issue intelligible to anyone over 16.)

Another recent book, dealing with the situation in various countries, is:

5. *The Breakdown of Money: An Historical Explanation.* C. Hollis. (Sheed and Ward.) 1934.

For a moderate statement of the "Social Credit" proposals of Major Douglas, containing a bibliography of the literature, see:

6. *This Age of Plenty.* C. Marshall Hattersley. (Sir Isaac Pitman and Sons.) 1929.

The following are the first and last books by S. A. Reeve:

7. *Cost of Competition.* S. A. Reeve. (New York: McClure, Phillips and Co.) 1906. Deals with the waste of effort in competitive "Commercialism".

8. *The Natural Laws of Social Convulsion.* S. A. Reeve. (New York: Dutton and Co.) 1933. Gives the theory of Wars and Revolution adopted in this book.

Silvio Gesell's System and Proposals will be found in:

9. *The Natural Economic Order.* Silvio Gesell, translated by P. Pye from 6th German edition (Neo-Verlag, Berlin-Frahnau), 1929.

10. *Free Money.* J. Henry Büchi. (Search Publishing Co.) 1933. 5.

11. *Stamp Scrip.* Irving Fisher. (Adelphi Co., New York.) 1933; Describes the sudden spread of Gesell's money in the U.S.A., and intended as a practical guide to municipalities wishing to adopt the new form of currency.

For information as to Technocracy:

12. *The A.B.C, of Technocracy,* Frank Arkright. (Hamish Hamilton.) 1933. is. td.

13. *What is Technocracy?* Allen Raymond. (McGraw Hill Book Co.) 1933. 65.

14. *The Engineers and the Price System.* Thorstein Veblen. 1921. Reprinted Viking Press, New York, 1934.

15. *The Economy of Abundance.* Stewart Chase [Macmillan and Co., New York]. 1934.

The frankest orthodox book on money (from the socialist standpoint) is:

16. *What Everybody wants to know about Money.* G. D. H. Cole and Eight Others. (Victor Gollancz, Ltd.) 1933. 5.

An excellent account of the early history of "banking" and the consequences of the Government's attempts to regulate it is:

17. *Industrial Justice through Banking Reform*. Henry Meulen. (R. J. James, Ltd.) 1917.

Two books about the present "Slump":

18. *Why the Crisis?* Lord Melchett. (V. Gollancz, Ltd.) 1931.

19. *The Truth about the Slump*. A. N. Field. P.O. Box 154, Nelson, New Zealand. 1932. (Privately printed.)

Some of the numerous writings of Arthur Kitson, the doyen of British Monetary Reformers, may be given:

20. *A Scientific Solution of the Money Question*. 1894.

21. *A Corner in Gold*. (P. S. King and Son.) 1904.

22. *A Fraudulent Standard*. (P. S. King and Son.) 1917.

23. *Unemployment. The Cause and a Remedy*. (Cecil Palmer.) 1921.

24. *The Bankers Conspiracy which started the World Crisis*, (Elliot Stock.) 1933.

Lastly a recent study of the doctrines of the New Economics:

25. *The Modern Idolatry. An Analysis of Usury and the Pathology of Debt*. Jeffry Mark [Chatto and Windus]. 1934.

Other titles

Omnia Veritas Ltd presents:

A classic work that exposes the fraudulent nature of the banking system and the huge and detrimental impact it has on all our lives.

PROMISE
to
P A Y
by
ROBERT MCNAIR WILSON

An inquiry into
The Modern Magic
called
"HIGH FINANCE"

The creation of money should be in the hands of the State or Head of Government and not in the hands of private banking.

Omnia Veritas Ltd presents:

The meaning of Monarchy's struggle against the Money Power

Monarchy *or* **M**oney
POWER
by
ROBERT MCNAIR WILSON

A **master-piece** of history

The true nature of Kingship revealed!

Omnia Veritas Ltd presents:

This meant creating, or making, money out of nothing, being allowed to call it money, and to lend it to the public at a high interest rate.

Fatima
and the
GREAT CONSPIRACY

This private syndicate acquiring a cast-iron monopoly over the supply and circulation of the money not just of England, but of the whole world...

OMNIA VERITAS

Omnia Veritas Ltd presents:

I wish to tell of the things which have happened to me in my struggle against the forces of darkness.

COLLECTED ESSAYS

EUSTACE MULLINS

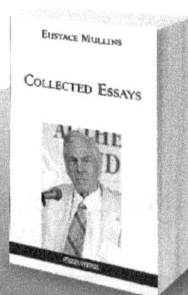

It is my hope that others will be forewarned of what to expect in this fight

OMNIA VERITAS

OMNIA VERITAS LTD PRESENTS:

CONVERSATIONS WITH JOHN F. KENNEDY

BY EUSTACE MULLINS

I engaged in lengthy disquisitions about the condition of man, the dangers apparent in his present estate, and what must be done to avert them...

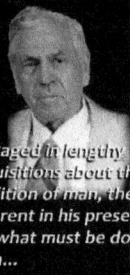

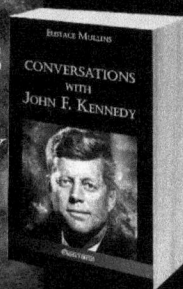

The martyred President of the United States

OMNIA VERITAS

Omnia Veritas Ltd presents:

Ezra's interest in money as a phenomenon, in contrast to the usual attitude toward money as something to get, is a legitimate one.

EZRA POUND

THIS DIFFICULT INDIVIDUAL

by EUSTACE MULLINS

An illustration for his own monetary theories...

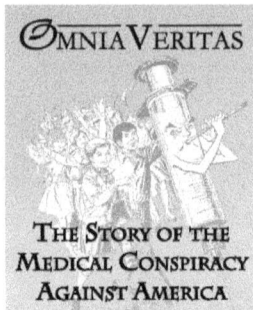

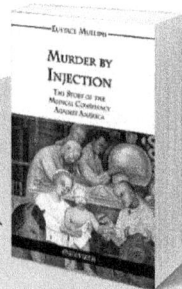

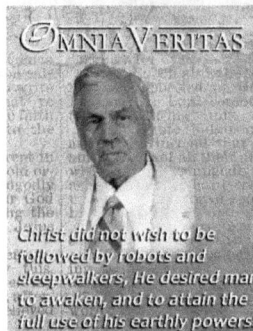

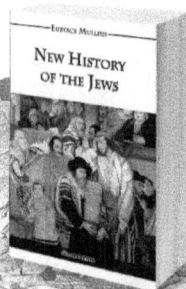

OMNIA VERITAS

Omnia Veritas Ltd presents:

THE CURSE OF CANAAN

A demonology of history

by

EUSTACE MULLINS

Liberalism, more popularly known as secular humanism, can be traced in an unbroken line all the way back to the Biblical "Curse of Canaan."

THE CURSE OF CANAAN
A demonology of history

Humanism is the logical result of the demonology of history

OMNIA VERITAS

Omnia Veritas Ltd presents:

THE RAPE OF

JUSTICE

by

EUSTACE MULLINS

AMERICA'S TRIBUNALS EXPOSED

SPIRIT OF JUSTICE

THE RAPE OF JUSTICE
AMERICA'S TRIBUNALS EXPOSED

American should know just what is going on in our courts

OMNIA VERITAS

Omnia Veritas Ltd presents:

THE SECRETS OF THE FEDERAL RESERVE

by

EUSTACE MULLINS

HERE ARE THE SIMPLE FACTS OF THE GREAT BETRAYAL.

THE SECRETS OF THE FEDERAL RESERVE
THE LONDON CONNECTION

Will we continue to be enslaved by the Babylonian debt money system?

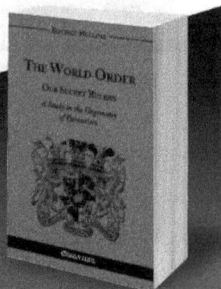